Paying It Forward

W9-AXW-681

The PhD Project:
Creating Tomorrow's Leaders in Business
Through Academe

by Ned Steele

Foreword by
Dr. Scott Cowen
President Emeritus, Tulane University

Introduction by
Bernard J. Milano
President, KPMG Foundation and The PhD Project

The PhD Project
Montvale, NJ

Paying It Forward
The PhD Project: Creating Tomorrow's Leaders in Business Through
Academe

Copyright © 2014 by The PhD Project

All rights reserved. No part of this book may be reproduced in any form whatsoever, by photography or xerography or by any other means, by broadcast or transmission, by translation into any kind of language, nor by recording electronically or otherwise, without permission in writing from The PhD Project, except by a reviewer, who may quote brief passages in critical articles or reviews.

ISBN: 978-0-578-14345-3

First Printing: July 2014
Printed in the United States of America

The PhD Project
Montvale, NJ

Contents

To view videos of these and other PhD Project doctoral students, professors and administrators, visit:

YouTube.com/thephdprojectvideos

Foreword

By Dr. Scott Cowen
President Emeritus
Tulane University

I am a great believer that if you invest in the right people, wonderful things can happen. I witnessed that first hand in 1993 when Bernie Milano, then head of college recruiting at KPMG, approached me with a novel idea. He asked me to lend my support for an initiative he and a handful of visionaries in the corporate and academic communities were establishing, The PhD Project.

When Bernie described the concept I didn't hesitate to express my enthusiasm. At the time I had been serving as dean of Case Western's Weatherhead School of Management for almost a decade and was all too familiar with the lack of diversity in business academia and corporate America. Luckily, soon after our initial conversations I was elected president of the American Assembly of Collegiate Schools of Business, now known as the Association to Advance Collegiate Schools of Business (AACSB). This allowed me to provide some concrete support as The PhD Project was taking its first steps in an environment that was ripe for change but also filled with skepticism.

Back in 1993 the idea of diversifying the faculty at business schools to many seemed like a more or less hopeless endeavor. For starters, there were concerns about whether the pool of qualified applicants who were willing to give up lucrative corporate careers was deep enough. Thanks to the relentless and deliberate work of The PhD Project, we now know that it can be done and that a diverse faculty attracts a diverse student body which ultimately leads to increased diversity and inclusiveness in the workplace and the boardroom. Since its inception, The PhD Project has made the mysterious and daunting process of pursuing a doctoral degree more tangible and accessible to hundreds of African-Americans, Hispanic-Americans and Native Americans.

As president of Tulane University for the last 16 years and someone who has spent the last 40 years as a faculty member and administrator in higher education, I can hardly overestimate the impact of diversity experiences on shaping the next generation of citizens and leaders. Enabling students to rub elbows with the real world—specifically people from a variety of backgrounds with different points of views, beliefs and ideas—means preparing students for success in a global society and a work environment that is more interconnected and complex than ever before.

At Tulane we have been particularly successful in expanding such learning experiences by embedding public service and community engagement into both our curricular and extracurricular offerings, but the transformative institutional changes that The PhD Project is promoting get to the root of the issue and surpass any diversity action plan that has been developed by individual universities. The PhD Project helps us create truly diverse management education programs where minority students are taught by role models, and all students, whether they are minority or not, benefit from learning in an educational setting that is reflective of the world they will live and work in after graduation.

Establishing The PhD Project was undoubtedly a fight worth fighting. I applaud those who have led the charge over the past 20 years with steady determination and those who took a leap of faith and became business professors as part of The PhD Project network. I note with satisfaction but not surprise that many of them have already received tenure, and some have gone on to become department chairs or assume other important administrative posts. At the risk of repeating myself, the impact of having a diverse business school faculty is profound; it touches every aspect of undergraduate and graduate education as well as our country's competitiveness and productivity.

To those of you who recently found their way to doctoral studies, congratulations on choosing a remarkably rewarding and stimulating career path. While the years leading up to your much longed-for title of "Doctor of Philosophy" may be rocky at times, as a participant in The PhD Project you can rest assured that you are not alone and that there is always someone to remind you that you have what it takes. Doing something that matters and approaching what you do with a can-do attitude is a winning combination. Just ask the founders of The PhD Project, and read this wonderful and inspirational story about how a few passionate and dedicated innovators can truly make a difference.

April 2014
New Orleans, Louisiana

Introduction

In 1994, KPMG Foundation, AACSB International, Citi Foundation and the Graduate Management Admission Council founded The PhD Project as a means to increase the pool of diversified candidates for positions in management by significantly increasing the number of minority role models and mentors in the front of the business school classroom. While our success in increasing the numbers of minority faculty and the qualitative impact on business education are documented, the personal connection we have with doctoral students, faculty, administrators and in many cases their families, has been the most gratifying.

On the following pages, you will read about the aggregate impact The PhD Project has had on doctoral students, faculty and administrators, who are not merely succeeding, but are collaborating and influencing each other and the next generation of business school faculty and corporate leaders. Their success stories—singly, but especially together—tell how this critical mass is helping to ensure success through the strong support network The PhD Project has created.

As the president of The PhD Project for the past 20 years, I am proud of this program's remarkable success and grateful for the time, talent and financial support it has received from so many corporations, professional and academic organizations and the over 1,200 minority faculty and doctoral students who have come through The PhD Project. We could not have come so far, and accomplished so much, without them.

However, the individuals whose stories are chronicled in this book, along with the hundreds that are not, are the true heroes and genuinely embody the term, "paying it forward." Their stories are inspiring, uplifting, encouraging and most importantly—true. We applaud them and wish them continued success on their journeys.

Bernard J. Milano
President, The PhD Project and KPMG Foundation

A Word From KPMG Foundation

K PMG Foundation is very proud to be one of the founders of The PhD Project along with Graduate Management Admission Council, AACSB International and Citi Foundation.

This journey started in September 1993, with 12 persons meeting in St. Louis to explore how to increase the diversity of business school graduates. That meeting was followed by several others, each time expanding the invitation list to enhance the input. The outcome of that process was a recognition that we had to attack the problem systemically. That led to a realization that there had to be a significant increase in the number of minority role models and mentors in the front of the classroom. Thus, The PhD Project was created.

KPMG Foundation has administered The PhD Project since its inception and continues in this role today, even after The PhD Project became a separate 501©(3) in July 2005. In addition to the administration, we are the principal funder, providing about one-third of the annual budget.

As further evidence of the success of The Project, academic organizations and individual colleges and universities provide about 50% of the current annual budget. This is a true collaboration of corporations, foundations and business higher education. And, as the stories in this book demonstrate, we are making a considerable impact on higher education and the business world as a whole.

I know I speak for all of us at KPMG Foundation when I say we are inspired, humbled and incredibly proud of each and every PhD Project professor, doctoral student and administrator. Through The PhD Project, we are creating a more dynamic business world, one that is truly representative of the world in which we live.

Jose R. Rodriguez
Chair, KPMG Foundation
KPMG LLP Chief Operating Officer - Global Audit

The PhD Project

The PhD Project is a catalyst for African-Americans, Hispanic-Americans and Native Americans to return to academia to earn their doctorates and become business professors.

When The PhD Project was created in 1994, there were only 294 doctorally qualified African-American, Hispanic-American or Native American professors in all U.S. university business schools. At press time in mid-2014, as The PhD Project marked its 20th anniversary of working to increase that number, there were more than 1,237 professors and 332 additional individuals working toward their doctorates.

The PhD Project's mission is to increase workplace diversity by increasing the diversity of business school faculty who encourage, mentor, support and enhance the preparation of tomorrow's leaders.

The PhD Project's vision is: a significantly larger talent pipeline of African-Americans, Hispanic-Americans and Native Americans for business leadership positions.

The main objectives of The PhD Project are to:

- inform and educate minorities about all aspects of a business doctoral program, and encourage them to follow their dream of becoming a professor;
- provide a nurturing support network for minorities as they navigate their doctoral program;
- increase the number of minority business professors who can function as role models and mentors;
- influence more minorities to pursue business degrees/careers;
- increase the number of qualified minority applicants to fill critical positions in the business disciplines;
- improve the preparation of all students by allowing them to experience the richness of learning from a faculty with diverse backgrounds; and
- reach the goal of a better prepared and more diversified workforce to service a diversified customer base.

The PhD Project uses a three-pronged approach to increasing the population of minority business professors:

- A marketing campaign to identify a population of the best and brightest potential PhD candidates of color via an extensive direct mail, print advertising and public relations campaign. Those who respond are invited to apply to The PhD Project annual conference.
- The annual conference. Each year, hundreds of applications to participate are received and reviewed. About 300 to 400 qualified applicants are invited to attend a two-day informational conference held each

November. There, participants hear from deans, professors and current minority doctoral students about the benefits and challenges of pursuing a business PhD. Candidates can meet with more than 80 doctoral-granting universities during a four-hour exhibit show at the conference. Many of these candidates are recruited before they even enter a program. They learn strategies to enhance their chances of finding an appropriate program and succeeding, and through intense interactions with academicians, typically gain a clear sense of whether "this is right for me" or not. This full immersion, it has been said, provides participants in two days with information and insights it would otherwise take them many months to acquire on their own.

- The Minority Doctoral Student Associations, formed by The PhD Project as a means of combating the traditionally high (25%) attrition rate inherent among all business doctoral students. Through these professional peer associations (in accounting, finance, information systems, management and marketing) minority doctoral students establish peer support relationships with others who are facing similar challenges on the way to becoming business school professors. Every minority business doctoral student in a full-time, AACSB-accredited program is a member of one of these associations. Each association has an annual conference held in conjunction with the relevant professional academic association. There, the PhD Project's doctoral students receive guidance and information concerning every step of the process of earning the doctorate and obtaining employment. The retention rate of doctoral students who are members of these associations exceeds 90%.

The PhD Project fulfills a societal need by providing underrepresented minorities with information about and access to, a career they might otherwise be unaware of. Likewise, The PhD Project fulfills an educational need by providing students with the opportunity to enrich their education through a diverse faculty. And furthermore, The PhD Project fulfills a workplace need by providing organizations with a larger pool of diverse applicants, while better preparing all applicants.

Origins:
How It Began

1

"*L ake Tahoe,*" thought doctoral student Michael
Clement. "*That's what I need. It's what we all need
right now.*"

The bracing Sierra Nevada breezes of Tahoe, just a few
hours' drive from the pressure cooker that is Stanford
University, seemed an ideal late summer cure for the grueling
1993-94 academic year he—and by extension his young
family—had just endured.
Endured, but perhaps not survived.
A highly regarded rising executive at Citibank, Clement
had dramatically shifted course a few years earlier. Gaining a
glimpse at the pinnacles of investment banking, he had paused
to reflect on the quality of life—and the impact on others—
his father had as a college professor. Contrasting the two
professions, Clement resigned from Citibank to enroll at
Stanford in the demanding five-year doctoral program that
would qualify him to become an accounting professor.
And, like countless other doctoral students before and
after him, he was stunned to learn just how demanding the
path was.

Nothing he had encountered in banking was as difficult. So tough that he and a fellow student had developed a private comedy routine to relieve the stress. Meeting by their mailboxes regularly, they would peer in to see if this was the day the dean had finally begun inquiring if they were ready to consider moving on to new endeavors.

"What were we thinking when we signed up for this?" Clement would ask his colleague.

"And what were *they* thinking when they let us in?" the friend would reply, as both men roared with laughter.

But alone, Clement wondered if this path was exceptionally difficult because he was a minority in a sea of white faces. It was a question he could not answer. There was no one to ask.

Clement didn't realize it then, but he was one of a handful of African-American doctoral students in accounting in the entire country. All of them, and likely their counterparts in all business discipline doctoral programs, were in the same boat—and struggling in it. Few people outside the inner circles of academe realized how difficult it was to earn a doctorate. The dropout rate was notoriously high. The lack of role models and mentors from a similar cultural background wasn't helping matters: back in the early 1990s, if you counted all the African-Americans who were accounting professors, you'd be counting a handful.

And then, in the spring of 1993, Clement had failed his comprehensive exams.

"Comps" are the last hurdle a doctoral student must clear before tackling the dissertation that leads to completion of the degree. And Clement had missed it.

Suddenly, the doubts he had always eased with his comedy routine could not be dispelled so readily. Serious thoughts about dropping the program and returning to business entered his mind.

A Lake Tahoe vacation between semesters looked like the ideal way to break from the stress, do some thinking and catch up on family time. Clement and his wife booked the trip.

And then, about a week before the departure date, Clement received an unexpected phone call from New York.

"I need you to attend a meeting in St. Louis two weeks from now," said Peter Thorp, an executive at Citibank whom Clement had worked with and admired.

Prepared to say no instantly, Clement listened further out of respect and loyalty. Thorp, who was heavily involved in Citi's charitable foundation and university relations, took several minutes to explain the situation.

Clement hung up the phone, wondering how to tell his wife that she'd be spending a few days of their long-anticipated Tahoe break alone with their baby son.

Zeroes...Zeroes...Zeroes. Dr. Theresa Hammond was dismayed by the consistency with which zeroes were appearing in the dozens of letters that filled her mailbox.

A white PhD in accounting who had once interned at a top global firm, Dr. Hammond had become interested in the relative absence of African-Americans in the accounting profession. Her interest filled first her 1990 dissertation and ultimately a book.

It had not been an easy road initially. Faculty and administrators at her university pressured her to abandon the topic. Puzzled at first—academia had historically supported equal opportunity—it took her a while to realize that major global accounting firms were significant funders of accounting education, and universities feared running any risk of offending them. Only one accounting professor had agreed to sit on the faculty committee to guide and judge her doctoral dissertation—a highly unusual state of affairs.

Undeterred, Dr. Hammond populated her committee with professors in other disciplines, even non-business ones. Their encouragement bolstered her resolve to continue on.

One of the scholarly works Dr. Hammond found in her research argued that students of color, in choosing a college major, were highly influenced by whether they knew a professor of color in that field—a potential role model and mentor.

With three degrees to her credit, Dr. Hammond had seen very few minorities standing in front of the classroom. Wondering if her experiences were unique, she wrote to 100 doctoral granting universities with three questions: How many African-American faculty do you have? How many African-American doctoral students? How many have you ever produced? This was when the letters full of zeroes began pouring in to her mailbox. Dr. Hammond had just found her next research topic.

It was 1991. Gathering a handful of names from her initial outreach, she wrote to each African-American doctoral student she had located and asked them to discuss their "unique concerns in attaining a doctorate." One of the candidates who responded was a second year doctoral student at Stanford University, Michael Clement, who invited Dr. Hammond to call him anytime she wished—anytime before 8 A.M.

The audit engagement had gone well, but an unsettling undertone emerged in the post-audit debriefing. The CEO of the public company, a prominent retailer with a heavily female customer base, looked over the conference table at the all-male team from KPMG and declared to them, "To understand our business, you need to understand our customer base."

KPMG immediately dispatched a star female audit leader from another state to join the team, and the engagement was saved. Word of the close call eventually reached the ears of the KPMG partner who headed KPMG's university recruiting program, Bernard Milano.

A KPMG lifer out of the Philadelphia office, Milano had been recognized by firm leaders for a combination, rare in the profession, of strong people skills and managerial strengths. They transferred him to run KPMG's far-flung nationwide campus recruiting system, which hired more than a thousand new graduates yearly. Ultimately, he rose to head all human resources functions for the firm.

His was a critical mission: in public accounting, where turnover of young employees is historically high, new hires are the lifeblood of a major firm's staffing function. Inside a firm like KPMG, the head of university hiring was one of the people considered most accountable for the ultimate success or failure of its junior associates.

Closely attuned to the social and business trends that drove corporate human resources, Milano was keenly aware in the early 1990s—a quarter century after the civil rights movement—that hiring a diverse work force was no longer a matter of affirmative action. With the U.S. population growing more diverse and business increasingly global, it was now a business imperative. The story of the unhappy CEO facing an all-male audit team was no great surprise to Milano. He had already been exploring ways to hire more women and underrepresented minorities, and had begun thinking deeply about why more African-Americans, Hispanic-Americans and Native Americans did not enter the profession. But the anecdote was the incident that snapped the firm to attention on the issue of diversity hiring. Milano noted that a tipping point had occurred. He foresaw that it might alter his priorities, not for firm hiring operations, but for his other responsibility: running the firm's charitable foundation.

A strategic leader and master networker, Milano understood that building deeper ties with business school academics would enhance his undergraduate recruitment efforts. As head of the KPMG Foundation, Milano oversaw a grant-awarding machine that generously supported academic research in accounting. Given the twin roles, he sat on numerous committees and boards of organizations connected with accounting and business education. Virtually any time that higher education and the accounting profession intersected, Milano was likely to be in the room. Traveling extensively to attend these meetings, he frequently saw the same faces seated around each table: corporate executives like him who hired college students, and representatives of the academic institutions that supplied them. Among this group, camaraderie and friendships developed amid the business meetings.

In coffee breaks and hallway chatter—and even occasionally on the formal agenda—talk sometimes turned to the dismally low rate of minority enrollment in business education. Many in the room, though deeply sympathetic to the goal, would throw up their hands in resignation and say they had tried everything they could think of.

Others would join Milano, shaking their heads in disbelief and disagreement. Among them was Theresa Hammond, now a professor at Boston College, who showed her emerging research on minorities in accounting education to Milano. Also in that camp was Dr. Melvin Stith, the energetic new dean of the business school at Florida State University, and a rarity as the African-American head of a prominent majority-serving business school. Another in that group was Milano's counterpart at KPMG client Citibank: an iconoclastic, bowtie-clad, blunt-speaking executive named Peter Thorp.

As many in this community were discovering, a growing body of research into the reasons for the scarcity of minorities completing higher education was emerging. From scholars like James Blackwell and Claude Steele, evidence was building that minority students were disadvantaged by stereotyping and the absence of role models and mentors who looked like them. This was especially so in business education: in the early 1990s, there were fewer than 300 doctorally qualified African-American, Hispanic-American or Native American professors in accounting, finance, information systems, management and marketing *combined, in the entire United States.*

So there were scant few role models for minority high school seniors to emulate and therefore few reasons to enroll in business school. Those who did enroll usually found no culturally attuned, simpatico minority professors to mentor them through the rigors of a Bachelor's program.

A change in thinking gradually took form. Until then, the academic establishment had shown little active interest in the racial makeup of its doctoral student bodies. "Affirmative action" and "equal opportunity" had been the bywords of diversity hiring for decades. Now, a new thought took hold: today's doctoral students are tomorrow's professors, role models, inspirations and mentors for generations of young people. *If we can attract more minorities to become business professors, we can attract more minorities to become business undergraduates.*

Diversify the front of the classroom, and you can diversify the rest of the classroom.
But how?

One early approach had emerged in 1989. Focusing on all five business disciplines, a group of academics and supporting organizations launched a Minority Summer Institute (MSI) at the University of Michigan.

Their plan was to attract a high-potential cohort of business undergraduates—minorities who were juniors and seniors—and offer them a content-rich summer exposure to a career in academia. The hope was that they would then pursue the career path to the professorate. Typically, this entailed a four to five year apprenticeship—the doctoral program—that provided the credentials needed to become a professor.

By all accounts, MSI was a well-designed and well-run program. But after four cycles, MSI had graduated 131 participants, yet produced just one doctoral program enrollee. Its disappointed organizers declared the effort a failure and shut it down.

It was the residue of this disappointment that infused much of the nay-saying Milano and Thorp were encountering in the early 1990s as they attended meetings with their academic cousins.

But there was no such defeatism in Tallahassee, Florida, where Mel Stith had become dean of the Florida State business school in 1991. On Dean Stith's agenda were to establish the four decade old undergraduate program as one of the nation's best and largest, build new facilities and multiply its endowment several fold. He would go on to accomplish all that and more, to the great satisfaction of his university. But he had another goal which did not at all initially please some.

Dr. Stith intended to significantly increase the representation of minorities in the doctoral program.

The faculty meeting actually grew heated. Doctoral student Mark Dawkins, permitted to sit in, was surprised by what he was hearing more than a quarter century after the civil rights era. Angry faculty members accused his mentor, Dean Stith, of lowering academic standards by admitting so many minority PhD students. "Do they mean *me?*" he wondered. "Do they mean my friends?"

The doctoral student's concern turned to admiration and respect for his mentor, as he watched Dean Stith disarm the opposition. Citing statistics and facts, he demonstrated that the overall performance on admissions exams of the school's minority doctoral students had been *higher* than those of the majority entrants. The issue was settled, and Florida State went on to become a national leader in attracting minority doctoral students. (Once when questioned by the university provost about his ambitious agenda in this regard, Stith had coolly replied, "If the football coach can recruit nationally, so can I."

Dean Stith's commitment to minority enrollment—and his success in meeting it—did not go unnoticed by Milano and Thorp. It was also duly noted and applauded by another African-American dean the businessmen had befriended: Dr. Quiester Craig, longtime head of the business program at North Carolina A&T University, one of the nation's leading historically Black universities (HBCUs).

A veteran of the early civil rights marches, Dr. Craig presented a genial country manner, sharp business acumen and a rock–solid determination to advance the cause of diversity in business education. His program did not grant doctorates in business, but he did hire faculty. The discovery that people in the business community were asking questions about faculty diversity was a thrilling one. If they succeeded, he could hire more African-American professors to teach his African-American students.

For years, Dr. Craig had been making the case among fellow deans for expanded minority representation at the doctorate and faculty levels at their predominantly white institutions. Most of the responses had consisted of platitudes, promises and excuses. The collapse of the MSI program had been a serious setback. Two businessmen suggesting to try something new? Dean Craig realized immediately that this time, his fellow deans would have to listen: *Big companies were a business school's customers.*

Craig saw the power of aligning with these men. From the start, he would be one of the strongest, most reliable sources of encouragement and information for not only the people who created The PhD Project but all of its doctoral students and professors.

And now, Mel Stith was demonstrating that increasing doctoral diversity was not Mission Impossible after all.

The two deans and the two businessmen also detected what they considered a potentially significant flaw in the MSI model. That program had targeted recent Bachelor's graduates—the cohort that historically populated business doctoral programs. Anyone much past their mid-20s was too old to become a professor, according to prevailing wisdom.

But the minority population was different.

In late 20th century America, business undergraduates from underrepresented minorities were typically first-generation college students. Inspired at some point in their youth to pursue a degree in business, they had enrolled in business school aiming to secure their slice of the American Dream—a position in Corporate America. Many came from underprivileged backgrounds in which no family member had ever gone to work in a corporate office. Virtually none had a parent, uncle or neighbor with a PhD in business to present the model of a career in academia. Many had overcome significant hardship and amassed considerable student loan debt in arriving at their senior year. And with the dream goal of a business career tantalizingly close, along came MSI to suggest an entirely different path.

So, Milano and his colleagues thought. *They've overcome obstacles and taken on debt to finally arrive at the cusp of the job they've dreamed of. Now someone proposes they stay in school five more years to get a degree they never heard of. No surprise that didn't work.*

Was there then no hope, they wondered at first.

And then Milano and Thorp thought of the countless enthusiastic young people entering their companies every year with high hopes, only to abandon the dream a few years later. For any one of numerous reasons, significant numbers of new recruits were growing dissatisfied with corporate life before mid-career. Moreover, women and minorities seemed especially vulnerable to this. For females, it was often the need for a family-friendly career that sent them looking for employment in other sectors. For minorities, it was frequently a growing desire to define satisfaction more broadly than by income—they yearned for the opportunity to serve their communities and impact more than a corporate bottom line.

That's the crowd that might want to become business professors, Milano and his colleagues realized.

But how? someone asked. *How do we reach them?*

2

Others were asking the same questions. AACSB, the body that accredits business schools and GMAC, the organization that conducts the GMAT test for business school admission, had sponsored the abandoned MSI program. Disappointed in its outcome, they remained greatly concerned about the lack of diversity in business schools—both on faculty and as students. A paper arguing for more inclusion written by the head of the Cornell University doctoral program, a white scholar named John Elliott, widened awareness and stirred deeper concern in the academic community. But no successor to MSI was emerging.

KPMG and Citicorp were far from alone among major global employers in calling on academia to develop a larger pool of minorities for them to hire. After a brief recession ended in 1991, the U.S. economy was entering its longest period of growth in history. The Internet and personal computing were igniting a great technology boom, with new companies and even new industries seeming to come alive daily.

And they were serving a customer base that was not only global but more diverse than ever. The U.S. Hispanic population was soaring at unprecedented rates. African-Americans, a generation after the civil rights era had opened opportunities, were attaining new levels of affluence.

Combining it all, corporate demand in the U.S. for skilled young workers from diverse backgrounds was ravenous.

There was another problem: by now, even the youngest Baby Boomers were established on career paths, and the generation following them was notably smaller. Supply was failing to keep pace with demand and, the experts warned, the imbalance threatened to place American business—and the country—at a disadvantage in the competitive global economy.

Companies responded, to greater or lesser success, by competing intensely against each other over available talent. Great sums of money and large amounts of energy were expended on a vast zero-sum game: none of this effort expanded the pool at all.

This was the backdrop that business school deans faced each day. The clamor to educate and graduate more business students—including students of color—was growing louder and more impatient. Employers were demanding it. The demographic trends were virtually dictating it. And a new generation of minority undergraduates was increasingly populating high prestige professions like law and medicine.

But they weren't coming to business school.

At AACSB, discussions grew more serious about how to inject diversity and inclusion efforts into the standards for accreditation. But, as one participant would recall two decades later, "It was just not something on the front burner. You would hear a lot of, 'We can't find them [minorities];

they are not interested. And a lot of the people that do come to us—well, they aren't capable of making it."'

Also concerned about the issue was the American Institute of Certified Public Accountants, better known as the AICPA. Public Accountants historically served their business clients with tax and audit services. But by the 1990s they were offering a rich mix of strategic and financial consulting services. These—unlike the cold numbers on a spreadsheet—required accountants to understand business practices and customer behaviors that were being permanently altered by increased diversity. The uncomfortable scene that had played out between the retailing CEO and his KPMG auditors was being echoed in other boardrooms.

Among the accountants thinking about these issues was a close colleague of Bernie Milano's. Robert Elliott (no relation to scholar John Elliott) had worked alongside Milano in KPMG's Philadelphia office early in both men's careers in the 1960s. (An office that was then, like so much of the profession, all white and all male.) The two men eventually were reassigned to different offices, but maintained a friendly rapport and stayed in frequent contact. Within the firm, and increasingly within the profession, Elliott was widely regarded as a visionary, a source of intellect with an uncanny ability to see, interpret and act on the big picture. In the early 1990s, he was an assistant to the chairman and sat on the firm's strategic planning committee. He was someone Milano liked to look to for insights and ideas.

So sharp were Elliott's intelligence and leadership strengths—he would ultimately become chairman of the AICPA—that he was establishing a national reputation. In 1992, the American Accounting Association (AAA)—the organization of accounting professors—honored him with its Wildman Medal Award, given annually for advancing theory and practice in their profession. The award carried a cash award of $2,500. Traditionally, recipients rolled the money back to the AAA. "I wanted to do something different," Elliott would later say.

Elliott had for some time been thinking about the interrelated issues of global competitiveness and diversity in business and access to education and educators as role models for minorities. Focusing on the dearth of minorities in accounting, he realized that while African-American youngsters might see African-American teachers and doctors in their communities, they weren't—as Theresa Hammond was documenting—seeing Black CPAs. At the time, 12% of the U.S. population was African-American, yet only 1% of CPAs were, while 4% of doctors were Black. "With no disrespect to my profession," he would later say, "it is a lot harder to become a doctor than a CPA... surely we could do better than 1%."

Rising to accept the Wildman Medal on August 11, 1992, Elliott explained that he was donating his cash award to create a new fund: one that would financially support the African-American doctoral students in accounting programs who would one day become professors.

But, he acknowledged, $2,500 would not go far to address the issue. And so he was triple-matching the amount to enlarge the pool to $10,000.

Still, he confessed, this was not much. Then he revealed the fruits of weeks of private discussions he had held with Milano and the leaders of the KPMG Foundation: KPMG would match the amount to make it $20,000.

"And," he told a now stunned crowd, "I'm very pleased that the AICPA will match that, bringing the total to $40,000."

That afternoon, the cause that Milano and Thorp had been discussing, prodding and debating privately with their cousins in the academy went public, with a highly visible program and funding to back it up. It would be just the beginning of a new era in the pursuit of greater diversity in business education.

The AICPA was to administer the two fellowships created from the fund Elliott had established, and it awarded them the following academic year. Still, an AICPA executive lamented to Milano and Elliott, it was a shame that more could not be done: other talented students had also applied for the fellowships.

"Send me their applications," Milano said. "I'll see if we can do something."

From the mid 1970s through the early 1990s, the KPMG Foundation had vastly expanded the body of academic accounting research by pouring millions of dollars into supporting worthy scholarly work. The program, hugely impactful, had been largely driven in its early days by Elliott.

"It's time to declare victory and close it down," Elliott said to Milano one day. "We have another issue to address.

"If we can do for diversity what we've done for research in auditing and tax," he said, "we will have made a lasting difference."

Milano agreed fully. The first outcome came a short time later. In autumn 1993, the trustees announced creation of a KPMG African-American Accounting Doctoral Students Scholarship program to fund some of the others who had applied to the AICPA. (It was later expanded to include Hispanic-Americans and Native Americans). Four recipients were identified and funded. What had begun as a $40,000 gesture of intent by Elliott now had the attention, backing and commitment of one of the accounting profession's global giants. The issue of diversity in business education was moving off the back burner and out of the cloistered hallways of academe, into the light of day.

3

Supporting current doctoral students in accounting would help those individuals and align with KPMG's interests. But it was a small dent in the larger challenge of attracting a vastly bigger pool of underrepresented minorities to become professors in all business disciplines. Only four African-Americans surfaced to qualify for the new KPMG scholarships. (Milano would soon meet a fifth, a doctoral student at Stanford named Michael Clement.) This paucity distressed him and the KPMG Foundation trustees, who stood ready to grant more scholarships—but had no takers.

A momentous decision resulted. The trustees authorized Milano to close their multimillion dollar spigot of support for research and divert the resources toward increasing faculty diversity. All of them accountants, and few of them with extensive experience in human resources or academia, they made one more decision: they entrusted Bernie Milano to figure out how to do it.

By now Milano had been on the circuit of academic meetings long enough and had met enough deans and department heads to grasp the landscape. Much of what he saw puzzled him. He observed that deans and department chairs largely stepped back from their doctoral programs, and especially from doctoral admissions, deferring to faculty groups to run these. As a result, if an institution had a strategic direction or priority, that institution had no high level leader to impart it to the doctoral program. Additionally, despite the increasingly apparent need to diversify their faculties, few university doctoral programs actively recruited students of any color: applicants were already plentiful. PhD programs were a small slice of a university's structure; they lacked meaningful marketing budgets. Anyway, universities did not seem to view the absence of doctoral student diversity with concern. Doctoral students were not a pipeline to diversifying their faculties: universities almost never hire their own graduating doctoral students. All in all, the dean had other things to care about.

This was the climate into which Milano had been thrust by his trustees with a mandate to create change. He may not have been a member of the academic club, but he had three other strengths: an outsider's ability to see things with a fresh eye, a businessperson's style of problem-solving and a good amount of KPMG money.

Milano did what any businessperson would do. He called a meeting.

St. Louis was, in September 1993, home to AACSB, one of the 1989-92 MSI program's sponsors. That connection, plus its central location, made it a logical choice to host what was in essence a summit meeting on diversity in business doctoral program admissions. With $5,000 supplied by KPMG and $5,000 from Citibank, Milano and Thorp rented a hotel conference room and invited many of the people they had been talking to over the past two years: deans, doctoral program heads, any African-American business professors they could locate, the former director of the MSI program, representatives of GMAC and other members of organizations concerned with the issue. There had not previously been such a group; the two men simply called people they respected. "It wasn't scientific," Thorp would later recount. "We just went and did it."

About two weeks before the meeting, Milano and Thorp realized they had forgotten something: an actual, live PhD student who was African-American living the life the meeting would address: someone who could relate the highs and lows of the experience and hopefully inform the group's thinking.

"There's a fellow who used to work at the bank with me," Thorp remembered. "Bright as anything. MBA from the University of Chicago. On track to go far. And then he left us to enroll in the accounting doctorate program at Stanford. Let's ask him."

Thorp picked up his phone and dialed his ex-colleague, Michael Clement. "Michael," he said, "I need you to attend a meeting in St. Louis."

Clement had not hesitated much in acceding to Thorp's request. Breaking away from his wife, son and their long-awaited Lake Tahoe vacation would not be fun for anyone. But he was excited by the thought that an influential group of people wanted to address the absence of African-Americans in the field in which he was, unbeknownst to them, now floundering.

Moreover, they wanted to hear what he had to say. And he was thinking about something that had troubled him all his adult life. Through his formative and early working years, he had known many smart, capable African-Americans failing to reach their career potential. One of the primary factors, he had noticed, was that they had no role models—an adult in their family or circle of friends—to encourage them to reach higher.

Clement needed to interrupt his vacation to fly to St. Louis and tell this group about… *his father*.

About a dozen representatives of various organizations had assembled in the meeting room of an airport hotel. After all the introductions had been made, and participant after participant shared their views on the diversity challenge, Milano turned to Clement and asked him to tell the group what it was like to be an African-American doctoral student.

Clement told them first about his father, who was a professor and the leading role model in his life. His dad, he explained, had motivated him more than anyone he had ever known, had emphasized the importance of education ever since he could remember and was one of the primary reasons for his success. He explained the difference between himself and other talented minorities he knew, whom he thought capable of becoming professors but wouldn't. He had a role model and they didn't. He told why he was entering academia: "I've seen my dad do things I thought were meaningful. I want to do something meaningful too."

He told them of his 80-year test: "When I get to be 80 years old and I look back on my career, what will I have done? Will I feel good about what I have accomplished?"

He spoke, too, about the challenges and loneliness facing an African-American student in an overwhelmingly white environment. One detail he did not mention was his recent failure at the comprehensive exams. This was because in reciting his 80-year test to this group, he felt his inner spark re-ignite. He knew then that he would return to Stanford, do whatever it might take to pass his "comps" and earn the degree. Therefore, there was no need to share this momentary setback with the group.

The group discussed, analyzed and debated all the issues all day, and into the next. It was clear that something had to be done, and there was enough energy and commitment in the room to make it likely that something *would* be done. Exactly what form that might take had not yet emerged. But having heard Clement tell his story, from a perspective they had not fully encountered before, they understood in a way they had not before, that creating role models was crucial to creating more minority graduates in business. "To increase minority representation among business school graduates, it is necessary to increase minority representation in the front of the classroom—the faculty," a written recap of the meeting later reported.

The group agreed to continue their discussions, reach out to others who might add new insights and ideas and reconvene in a few months.

Re-energized, Clement returned to his vacationing wife and son, and then back for the semester to Stanford, where he signed up for supplemental math classes. These would enable him to pass his exams the following spring, go on to earn his PhD and become a respected professor at the University of Texas, Austin (see For Everyone Who Comes After You).

Leaving the St. Louis hotel he thought, "Whatever this group decides to do, it will probably happen five or 10 years from now."

Being businesspeople, Milano and Thorp did not understand the concept of something taking 10 years. And Milano left the meeting with a different takeaway after hearing Clement's story. *"Here's someone who gave up a nice home and a great job at Citibank,"* he mused. *"He was appointed by the CEO to sit on company task forces. He gave that up to become a professor—and his wife was pregnant.*

"If someone like Michael Clement would give up all that for this...there must be others."

4

Carolyn Callahan endured in silence the indignity of being pushed in a wheelchair through bustling Newark Airport. Fiercely independent and highly accomplished as a scholar, she was not happy about being transported in this manner. But she knew she was simply not capable at that moment of getting from gate to taxi on her own power.

Just a few weeks earlier, she had undergone major surgery to resolve a potentially life threatening condition. Arguably, she should not have been traveling at all. But she had made it this far, from South Bend, Indiana where she was a rising star on the accounting faculty of Notre Dame, and she was determined to reach Montvale, New Jersey.

Montvale, about an hour from New York City, was where KPMG based many of its support functions, including the university recruiting and charitable foundation activities that Bernie Milano directed. It was March 24, 1994, about six months after the St. Louis meeting, and much had transpired since then. Throughout the late fall and early winter, ideas and suggestions had flown over the phone lines and fax machines of the St. Louis group and its widening circle. That January, about 20 of them had met in Montvale amid a brutal winter storm that stunned the attendees from Southern states into vowing they would never again set foot in New Jersey in winter. That session had led to the call for this larger meeting. The calendar declared it the third day of spring: January participants, Southerners included, returned—and with them nearly 20 more newcomers—to the emerging initiative.

On one hand, Dr. Callahan might have been inclined to dislike the KPMG Foundation's decision to shut down its large scale funding of accounting research: she had been one of the beneficiaries of this mainstay program. But she was an African-American woman, risen from poverty to achieve a position in academia that few others of her background had. Upon hearing that a group convened by her benefactor wanted to examine the struggles of African-Americans in business academia, Carolyn Callahan dismissed any health concerns and booked a flight to New Jersey. When she arrived at the KPMG complex in Montvale, she walked directly to the front row and sat right in the middle of it. Looking around her, she could not believe that this many people cared enough about diversity in business school to be present. For years, as an African-American woman, she had felt utterly alone.

The January Montvale meeting had been noteworthy, and not only for the epic winter storm (which had stranded some participants, and which the *New York Times* labeled in a headline the "Worst Possible Combination of Rain, Sleet and Snow") The formal recap of that meeting said that the day "may well have generated more questions than it answered." But, the report added, "Certainly, we all came away with a new awareness of the scope of the problems confronting minority students at the doctoral level."

This, in itself, was a milestone. Senior people in academia and business had not thought about and discussed such thoughts before to this extent.

By the March meeting, KPMG and its Foundation were moving toward two goals: creating a national organization for African-American doctoral students in accounting, and creating a "National Committee to Recruit African-Americans into Accounting Doctoral Programs." At this meeting, similar concerns regarding all five business disciplines were on the table. In the conference agenda binder, on a chart captioned "What can you do?" was this entry: "Support formation of a national organization for African-American PhDs."

Accompanying Dean Stith to Montvale was the fourth year doctoral student who had watched him stare down prejudice in his department, Mark Dawkins. Dawkins joined Clement, who had come in from California, and other doctoral students to help the larger group understand what made them tick: what had motivated them, what in their backgrounds had prepared them, what obstacles and challenges stood in their path and how they were handling them. The four students who had received the scholarships KPMG had created a few months earlier (a fifth was awarded to Clement on the day Milano met him in St. Louis) sat on a panel and told their stories.

Among them was Sandra Shelton, in the final year of her doctoral program at the University of Wisconsin, Madison. For four years, until the day she was invited to join Dawkins, Clement and the others, she had believed that she must be the only African-American PhD candidate in accounting anywhere in the country.

Dr. Callahan and the African-American doctoral students present listened attentively as the mostly white academic crowd engaged in soul searching over what they could do differently, and additionally, to increase minority enrollment.

When Dr. Callahan finally rose to speak from the floor, she recounted her own story: born in poverty to a factory worker and a domestic, she had excelled with numbers and was driven to succeed in accounting. Deciding to become an accounting professor, her skills and talent clearly visible, she had nonetheless encountered skepticism and prejudice in academia—far more than she had in the business world. She spoke eloquently and in detail of the extraordinary isolation and alienation she had experienced as a doctoral student. Despite support from her business school, "it felt like the loneliest place in the world" for an African-American woman, she recounted. When something went against her, she could not tell if it was something typical of everyone's doctoral experience or because of her identity. And which identity: as a female, a mother, an African-American?

It was clear, from what she and the doctoral students recounted, that the rising desire to increase minority enrollment presented a serious dilemma: if the effort succeeded, it would drive minorities into an environment and career path that could traumatize some of them, if not lead them to failure.

This, Milano knew, could not be allowed to happen. When Dr. Callahan finished speaking, he declared, "We are going to fix that."

"How?" asked Dr. Callahan.

"I don't know yet, but I promise you that we will," Milano responded.

Although it wasn't yet apparent, this was the moment when the PhD Project Doctoral Students Associations, a linchpin of the program's component to prevent doctoral dropouts, were born.

Also riveted by every word Dr. Callahan spoke was Sandra Shelton, the doctoral student from the University of Wisconsin - Madison who had been overwhelmed to learn she was not the only African-American in the country pursuing an accounting doctorate.

Now, a second revelation opened to her: not only were there others like her, *but here was someone who had actually overcome the extreme challenges Shelton and the other doctoral students were currently experiencing.* Moreover, Dr. Callahan had not merely survived, she was now an academic star!

The PhD Project did not yet exist, and it had not been named. But as Shelton listened with fascination to Dr. Callahan, it had just created its first moment—of many to come—in which a successful African-American business professor rose to inspire someone who would become one.

Like, Dr. Callahan, Shelton had grown up in the South and was now ensconced at a Midwestern university. Here indeed was someone she could relate to. At the next meeting break, she approached Dr. Callahan, and the two women bonded on the spot. They would go on to advance the friendship by phone after returning home. The following year, when newly minted Professor Shelton needed help in preparing for her first formal scholarly presentation, she drove out to South Bend to gain Dr. Callahan's insights. From then on, until this day, Dr. Shelton would reach out for counsel from Dr. Callahan at significant moments in her career.

The PhD Project did not exist, and its first meeting was nine months away, but it had just created its first lifelong mentoring relationship.

Shelton would recall the Montvale meeting more than two decades later as "a life-changing moment for me." The PhD Project, still just a concept without a name, was months from lifting off the ground. But it had already changed two lives: Michael Clement's, at the St. Louis meeting, and now Sandra Shelton's.

At one point in the session, one of the white academics asked Shelton to explain why putting more African-American professors in front of classrooms would change things. The answer expected by those already steeped in the issues was that minority students needed role models and mentors. Shelton went in another direction: "Having an African-American professor benefits all students," she said. "All students have to realize that we can all learn from someone who is of a different background. If students want to succeed in business, they will need to respect the opinion of others who are different from them." The initiative they were developing, the group saw, would benefit *all* students.

While many ideas and possible directions swirled among the participants as they dispersed, Milano and Thorp began sharpening the focus and identifying the challenges: a national program was needed to draw more minority applicants to business doctoral programs. It would need a support component to ensure that those who took the leap would not succumb to the pressures and loneliness that awaited them. An effort of this magnitude would need the buy-in of deans and doctoral programs, to make sure the new wave of minority applications would be considered seriously.

And, they realized, to gain buy-in at a high enough level within the universities to have an impact, the effort would have to focus on all five business disciplines, not only accounting. There were isolated, overstressed doctoral students in management, marketing and the other disciplines. And they were from all three underrepresented groups. The new program would have to include Hispanic-Americans and Native Americans as well.

Finally, because they were businesspeople, they saw something else: the best way to attract more minority applicants to PhD programs was to launch a full scale marketing program, one that would target tens of thousands of early and mid-career minority professionals in the business world by direct mail and media advertising. One that would show them, Madison Avenue style, the many benefits of a career as a professor.

This was beginning to sound ambitious—and considerably more costly than KPMG and Citibank could cover alone. Probably more than could be accomplished even with AACSB and GMAC joining in generously. Milano tentatively committed KPMG to launch the still undefined program with $250,000; Thorp added $50,000 from Citibank.

The two by now each had an extensive Rolodex filled with their counterparts at other corporations. All were playing variations of the same game: networking in and around higher education, to simultaneously offer their company's resources and enhance their college hiring programs. These were executives from the nation's best-known businesses, and Milano and Thorp were seeing them at meetings where business education and diversity were Topic A. The two men started approaching them with an unusual proposition: would they consider investing in a new program to increase diversity in the work force, by increasing diversity of faculty to attract those future workers to business school and then mentor them through it?

It was a proposition initially hard to grasp: most in this group enthusiastically funded programs centered around MBA, undergraduate and even high school minority students. These investments usually produced direct return on investment in the form of student interns they could hire and develop for future employment. Hearing of this new idea, their immediate response was invariably the same: "Where's the ROI? We don't hire PhDs."

Finding corporate partners for this initiative would not be a snap. Only companies truly interested in permanently altering the landscape, or far-sighted enough to look into the future, were likely to commit.

Nonetheless, Milano knew those companies existed.

It was also apparent that Hispanic-Americans and Native Americans were experiencing the same isolation and challenges that African-Americans were. An extreme example of this was a first-year student in Dean Stith's information systems department at Florida State, Laura Hall.

With three little girls aged one to five and a marriage that was ending, Laura Hall was up to her eyeballs in debt and stress when she entered the doctoral program. She had been advised—by one of her favorite professors, at that—that she shouldn't even try.

Supplementing her small teaching assistant stipend with tutoring for $15 an hour, she was finding the financial pressure alone to be "a total nightmare not counting working on a PhD and taking care of three girls." She felt as if each day she was stuck on a treadmill running at full speed morning to night.

5

That spring, as Milano and Thorp made their customary rounds of meetings with academic groups, they shared an idea that had gained momentum during the Montvale sessions: a national conference to assemble all those African-Americans, Hispanic-Americans and Native Americans who would be responding soon to the still-to-be created and funded marketing campaign that would sell them on a career in academia.

Before buying into the notion of abandoning a six-figure corporate salary for five years as an impoverished doctoral student, the two men realized, this group would need to learn far more than an ad or mailer could convey. A conference where experts in the field could lay out the whole idea and all its ramifications, warts and all, seemed necessary. But asking this group to spend several hundred dollars to attend such a meeting would be like charging a customer to walk into your store. Sponsors would have to foot the whole bill.

Academics hearing this proposition generally reacted with out-loud laughter.

The whole idea was pointless, some would gently remind the two, because of its flawed premise: The reason few minority business professors existed was clear, they said: business schools were not turning out new minority PhDs. The reason for that was also clear: minorities weren't applying to doctoral programs. They just weren't interested in getting a business PhD or were not qualified to, a few leaders of the academy felt compelled to remark in private.

A banker and an accountant are two very different creatures. But one trait they share is that nothing fires up their determination like being told they don't know what they are talking about. And confidence in their vision was further rising in Milano and Thorp when Sandra Shelton's dean at Madison, Andrew Policano, and two doctoral program directors emerged to join Deans Craig and Stith in support of the plan: John Elliott of Cornell and Ralph Katerberg of the University of Cincinnati. Katerberg enthusiastically offered to help the fledgling effort in any way he could. Privately, though, he wondered whether the whole idea might be too ambitious to fly. Things that big just didn't happen that quickly in higher education.

So when a small group began conceptualizing what a meeting of prospective doctoral students from underrepresented minorities might look like, one academic said, "Yes, we have to do a conference—maybe next year."

"No," Milano said. "This year."

A short time later, back in Montvale, Milano stopped by the desk of one of his KPMG Foundation team members. "We're going to hold a big meeting, and I'd like you to organize it," he told her.

"What kind of meeting? Who's coming? What's it about?" Tara Perino asked.

Milano confessed that he could not yet answer any of these questions. But he assured her that he shortly would. "And I do know that I need you to make it happen," he added.

KPMG's college recruiting unit had to compete with five global accounting giants and scores of public companies to attract the best talent on campus each spring. Accordingly, it directed an extensive marketing and advertising effort toward those students. One day, Milano called Beth Donahue, the principal of the ad agency behind it, into his office. He proceeded to explain his emerging new initiative. Could she develop a campaign to market a career in business academia as impactful as the one that marketed KPMG to accounting students? Intrigued and excited, Donahue assigned her top writer and designer to the assignment. First, she reminded her client, the initial step in advertising was branding.

About two weeks later she returned with a name. Its simplicity belied its power. It connoted, as Donahue would later recall, a long-term effort, built on the contributions of many people with diverse backgrounds and strengths that would evolve and expand over the years with the expectation of becoming self perpetuating.

There were just three words on the display board she placed on an easel:

The PhD Project.

She then lifted out another board, and this one bore a dazzling image: a bright rainbow-colored tassel, affixed to the corner of a mortarboard graduation cap. It would become the signature image of The PhD Project, conceived, Donahue would explain many years later, in "a moment of graphic clarity and genius."

Calling in an ad agency to create logos, slogans and ads for a six-figure media campaign was decidedly not something business doctoral programs in higher education were accustomed to. But among the many in that community who genuinely yearned to see greater diversity in their midst, recognition grew that it might be time for a new approach. They had done it their way—the MSI was a well-funded culmination of their efforts—and had not moved the needle. Now, thanks to the financial commitment and marketing mindset that business was injecting, the pieces of this newly-named PhD Project were magically coalescing into a mosaic no one had imagined before—outreach to a more mature target audience, a well-funded advertising campaign and a conference to promote the very career path they themselves had chosen. More and more business academics began to think that it might be worth a try.

As the plan for a big national conference took shape, it focused on large amounts of information delivery. A few dozen members of the higher education community—deans, department chairs, faculty and current doctoral students—would be needed to pull back the curtain and reveal some of the hidden mysteries of how academia works that were hidden from the world at large. What exactly did a professor do? What was scholarly research and how did it get done? What was the daily life of a professor like? What were the disciplines within business study, and what were the career prospects within them? What were the secrets to crafting a successful doctoral program application? What did it cost to leave a business job and become a student again? What about the family issues? And what might it be like to encounter all these issues as the only representative of a minority group in the business school?

These, and many more, were questions that could only be answered by those who were living the life. Dr. Callahan and others were dispatched to reach out to anyone who might be willing to help. To Chapel Hill and Arizona State, to Texas A&M and M.I.T, to Austin and Ann Arbor—anywhere they knew anyone who might be willing, they reached out. There remained the question of when to hold the conference. Summer was approaching, and an entire ad campaign was yet to be devised and rolled out. Milano and Thorp, involved heavily in so many professional and nonprofit organizations, swiftly put together a list of all the groups with large membership lists of minorities in business, or interested in business. These individuals would be the campaign's target audience. Milano and Thorp worked the phones incessantly to secure pledges from dozens of such groups to lend their mailing lists to the direct mail campaign. These organizations were dubbed "The Supply Alliance." An ad buy for media advertising was put in place; direct mail pieces went into design.

The admissions calendar for doctoral programs dictated that the conference be held no later than mid-December if it was to impact the 1995-96 admissions cycle. This was not much time to carry out a campaign or arrange a meeting. Geography and cost suggested Chicago as the location. Now that Tara Perino knew the purpose and location of the meeting she had been asked to arrange, she and her team turned to their first challenge: finding an airport hotel that could accommodate a two and a half day conference that December 14 through 16, perhaps for several hundred people. Or perhaps not: No one organizing The PhD Project's first marketing campaign and conference yet had any real idea of how much response they would receive.

Nor had a clear strategy emerged for attracting the additional funding, from other companies and organizations, that would be needed to cover the costs of the marketing campaign followed by full travel and hotel expenses for several hundred. Milano and Thorp had just been calling people they knew.

One day, Milano telephoned Thorp, as alarmed as it was possible to be over exceptionally good news:

"Peter! Chrysler wants in! What do we tell them? How much do we ask for?"

There was no strategic or fundraising plan to offer an answer. There was no alternative but to improvise.

The two men agreed that the fledgling organization needed reasonably substantial contributions. They also realized, with time short, that asking for too much would backfire: large grants required a corporate foundation's board approval, and these boards met infrequently. Fortunately, both Milano and Thorp were themselves in the business of running a corporate foundation and were easily able to identify the sweet spot: a contribution of $25,000 was meaningful enough to make a difference and small enough that a staff director could approve it without board approval.

Milano called back the Chrysler representative to request $25,000. In a few weeks, a check in that amount bearing the company's iconic five-sided star logo arrived. The PhD Project had its first new corporate sponsor to add to the four founding sponsors.

6

Milano's spontaneous promise to "fix" the problem that Carolyn Callahan had exposed in Montvale—that new doctoral recruits would need peer and mentor support to get over the many hurdles of earning the degree—turned out to be simple, conceptually, to keep.

There were, KPMG determined after several months of outreach and research, just 42 African-American accounting doctoral students in the country. (Hispanic-Americans and Native Americans would be added the following year, after The PhD Project was formally launched to target all three groups.)

It would be relatively easy and affordable to host a meeting for them all in Montvale during summer break. As an added bonus, the national organization of accounting educators, the American Accounting Association, was holding its annual meeting in nearby New York City that summer. It wouldn't take much more to give the African-American students a bonus rarely available to doctoral students of any background: entrée to the conference, where they could network with not only the field's leading scholars, but with potential future employers.

KPMG announced formation of the African-American Accounting Doctoral Students Association and invited all 42 to attend its first meeting in Montvale, and the AAA conference. All expenses were to be covered by the KPMG Foundation. Also invited: a score of experienced accounting professors and scholars to meet, inform and mentor the student invitees. It was an offer too good to refuse; 35 of the 42 showed up.

That August 1994 inaugural meeting of what would become the PhD Project Accounting Doctoral Students Association meeting would never have occurred, it was later agreed, had Dr. Callahan not recounted the painfully personal story of her doctoral experience six months earlier. "It would have taken us years to figure out why we were having a high dropout rate," Milano later mused.

The meeting opened on a series of emotional high notes that echoed the emotional moment six months earlier in the same building, when Sandra Shelton had first met other African-American doctoral students. In this pre-Internet, pre-Facebook era, African-American doctoral students were unconnected to each other, and generally unaware of each other's existence. Most of the 35 attendees thought exactly the same thing upon entering the meeting room: "I can't believe this. I used to think I was the only one."

Michael Clement would later say of that moment that he felt like someone who had long been searching for the right congregation to join: "I felt as if I'd found the church that I'd been looking for."

Networking and mentoring commenced; important information and insights were imparted; lifelong bonds were started. At the meeting's conclusion, each member of the group affixed their signature to a charter document commemorating the occasion. The charter today hangs on a wall at the KPMG complex in Montvale.

After two days, the group headed en masse to the AAA meeting in New York. Walking into the conference as a group, they spied at the other end of the meeting hall a tall African-American man standing alone. None of them knew him. It was hard to tell who was more startled: the group, upon discovering they had apparently overlooked someone, or the man, whose initial thought was, *"What is this about, and why wasn't I invited to the party?"*

The man turned out to be Peter Johnson, a CPA who was teaching accounting without a doctorate in a non-research university in Hawaii. Johnson, attending his first AAA meeting, hadn't really wanted to pursue a PhD; he felt happily situated. Very quickly, he was invited to join the party, and from that moment was part of the group. Within a short time his new friends were extolling the benefits of academic life that he was missing as a non-doctoral instructor.

By the end of the AAA meeting, Johnson was seriously considering, for the first time, plunging in fully and earning his doctorate. The PhD Project, still not yet fully launched, had just scored its first recruit.

The model for the PhD Project Doctoral Students Association, of which there would eventually be five, had just been designed and tested—though no one fully realized it at the time.

7

September in San Francisco is a refreshing antidote to a punishing East Coast summer. The cool breezes can clear out mental cobwebs and awaken brain cells dulled by months of heat and humidity back home.

Perhaps this explains why an idea suddenly hit Bernie Milano as he strolled the exhibition floor at the National Black MBA Association's annual conference. At his side were Dean Stith and two GMAC executives, Julie Dolan and Nicole Chestang.

Milano had not attended this organization's conference before. But now he was formally the head of The PhD Project, and a convention full of African-Americans holding MBAs was a room filled with his target market. The ad campaign to reach them had recently launched, and it was just three months before the big inaugural conference.

But the exhibit hall baffled him. It was filled with booths and displays from most of the country's major universities, and they were promoting their MBA programs. Milano said to his colleagues, "This is a national convention of people who already have MBAs. Why are business schools here to sell them what they already have?"

The group explained that many attendees at conferences like this were young business executives still thinking of getting an MBA. "Oh," Milano thought. "Just like our conference will be for people thinking of going for a PhD."

"We need these schools at our conference too," he declared to his colleagues. "Their doctoral programs have to bring their booths. Let's invite them and charge them a fee to recruit our people."

Stith, who had stood steadfastly by Milano for months as some of his peers had dismissed and even ridiculed the idea of The PhD Project, could not resist a chuckle.

Stith proceeded to explain, in the manner a teacher might when the class's brightest student commits an uncharacteristic blunder, that doctoral programs didn't have to recruit: they had far more applicants than open slots. They were too small to have recruiting budgets. And, the *coup de grace*: "Bernie, we're business schools. We like to *get* money from guys like you, not *give* it."

To which Milano replied, "Well, everything we've done so far has been something people told us wouldn't work. Why don't we try one more thing that won't work?"

It was, he had to admit, late in the game to add a university recruiting fair to the program. December was practically around the corner, the academic year was under way and doctoral program budgets and travel schedules for the year had been set. Moreover, the conference had been announced to the world: full page color ads had run in *Black Enterprise*, *Minority MBA* and other publications. Mailers were going out to thousands in the targeted demographic. The decision had been made to build in a rigorous applications and admissions function: only those who appeared to possess the credentials and strengths a doctoral program required would be allowed to attend the all-expenses-paid event.

A 10-page paper application had been distributed. Ralph Katerberg had agreed to assist Milano in evaluating the applications that were beginning to trickle in. (In later years, the process would be formalized with Deans Stith and Policano and Dr. John Elliott joining). The Hyatt O'Hare had been booked for the event. A steering committee of sponsors and academics, ranging from Dean Policano to doctoral students like Sandra Shelton, was busily working out an agenda and lining up the panelists and presenters who would populate it.

Yes, it was late, but it was never too late to get it right. Soon after Milano departed San Francisco, a letter went out from Montvale inviting 100 doctoral granting universities to send representatives to Chicago on December 15th and 16th.

One other challenge remained, and it played out largely out of view of the principal sponsors and leaders. Many African-Americans, exemplified by Clement and Shelton and the 33 others that attended the AADSA meeting, were powerfully impacted by the opportunity to meet and network with peers and mentors of a similar background. But as some of the conference planning group reached out across academe to spread the word and solicit speakers for the conference, a pushback developed. It came from a segment of the African-American community of business scholars. Looking with skepticism at an outside group—seemingly led by white men from multinational businesses—entering their arena with seemingly substantial money in hand, they asked pointed questions. What did these businesspeople really know about the African-American experience in academe? Why, this contingent asked, should we join their game?

"There was a group of African-Americans who felt we should go off and do this by ourselves, and it should be a separate sort of vehicle," Dr. Callahan recalled many years later. "There was a strong component to that.

"There was another group—and it was smaller—that said, 'No, we need to be an integral part of the profession.'".

Dr. Callahan, who held the respect of both camps, put in many hours to spread her message: "Everybody needs to come to the party." It would take time to bring everyone under the tent: even several years later, with the Project and its Doctoral Students Associations well established—and with doctoral students enjoying the benefits of them—doubts lingered. Information Systems Professor Laura Hall, one of the earliest and strongest supporters of The PhD Project, heard it: "The first few years some of the students were suspicious of The Project. They didn't understand what the Project wanted from us and thought they may be expected to go to work for KPMG or owe some other kind of debt."

Dr. Hall, who worked to dispel that suspicion, nonetheless could understand where it was coming from when seen in the context of the underrepresented minority experience in business education. "After all," she explained, "there was no other such organization where people wanted to help people of color."

8

Mel Stith felt excitement rising in him as he stood by the registration counter and watched the people arrive. First in a small trickle, then in clumps and then in a crowd they came. *"Yes, this is going to be something special,"* he thought.

It was the evening of December 14, 1994, and the scene playing out before him was the one many of his colleagues had told him could never happen.

It was the opening session of the first PhD Project conference. For months, those colleagues had told him this would be a fruitless cause: there simply weren't enough African-Americans, Hispanic-Americans and Native Americans interested in abandoning successful business careers to become doctoral students.

Now those supposedly disinterested people were showing up—forming lines and crowding the welcome reception.

It wasn't a surprise to Dean Stith at this stage: The Project had been tracking the numbers ever since the first applications had started trickling in. Mailing out thousands of flyers, launching an ad campaign, renting out a hotel: the planning group had done all this not knowing who would be proven wrong—the skeptics or themselves.

It was, in hindsight, an audacious and very large gamble.

But it was one based on considerable conviction, thought and planning. In the end, hundreds of those supposedly disinterested people had expressed interest. In all, 570 had completed the formal application process. Exactly half— 285—had been evaluated as doctoral program-ready and invited to attend the conference, all expenses paid.

Stith knew these numbers. But it was this moment, as the numbers turned into live human beings standing before him, when it became real.

They arrived at all levels of expectation: already applying to doctoral programs, seriously interested but not yet sure it was for them, considering it for the first time... or merely curious.

They came for many different reasons: some had always known they would someday teach college and some had grown frustrated or disillusioned with their current career path. Some were seeking a profession that enabled flexibility for time with family. Some had been amazed to learn they could get paid to pursue research in whatever interested them. All but 19 of the 285 invitees showed up, and so there were 266 reasons why they came.

But here they were, at this airport hotel, and there would turn out to be many more like them: this first conference was to become an annual affair, each in late fall drawing an even larger number of people to consider life as a business professor. Through the remainder of the 1990s, into the 2000s and the 2010s, they would keep coming, burying the myth that they didn't exist.

And they would return home from the conference to process it all. Some, having gotten the up-close look, would decide it was not for them, and this too was a success. Now that they knew, a nagging curiosity had been eliminated; they were free to concentrate on the career they were in. Others would dash off applications immediately. Some would take a more measured path, studying their options further.

And after they reached their decision, many would apply to and enter doctoral programs. Four, five or six years later they would emerge as professors, in numbers previously unimagined, until by 2014, 20 years later, they had more than quadrupled the number of African-American, Hispanic-American and Native American professors of business.

"Yes, this is going to be something special," Dean Stith thought as the crowd began filing in to the hotel that night in December 1994.

Dozens of minority business faculty and current doctoral students from across the country were arriving too, having taken time off from their work to provide the insights and information that the 266 applicants had come to hear.

Among them was Laura Hall, the struggling single mother from Florida State who didn't know, day to day, if she would survive her doctoral program. Getting to the conference had been a minor miracle, and she had done so only at the urging of Dean Stith. Although all expenses for the conference were covered, she still had to pay $100 for child care for her three little girls, "which might as well have been $1,000" given her financial straits. And she had neither a credit card nor pocket cash for tips and incidentals.

But she was there.

The pushback Dr. Callahan had initially encountered from some had been dissolved by a growing wave of enthusiasm and excitement. Long having felt the isolation of their status, many faculty and doctoral students were emotionally overcome to see, upon entering the welcoming reception, more than 300 people who looked like them and either shared their profession or aspired to.

Representatives of the four founding sponsors—KPMG, Citibank, AACSB and GMAC—were present to see the fruits of their efforts in person. They were joined by Chrysler and a second new sponsor, Texaco.

Also on hand were representatives of 67 degree granting colleges, having come to staff the recruiting tables that Stith had told Milano would never be filled. As promised, Milano had returned from the September meeting of Black MBAs to invite every university with a doctoral program. Soon, 33 colleges had accepted the offer, a handful had declined and dozens more had simply not responded.

To that large group, Milano sent a second letter thanking them for considering the invitation. And, oh yes, he added, we thought you'd like to know who of your colleagues will be joining us. He attached a list of the 33 schools that would attend.

Within days, 34 more colleges had hastily written to say that they would be there too.

The conference opened formally the following morning, with 300 people filling a meeting hall—a sight that brought tears to the eyes of some veteran faculty members who had served for years, decades in some cases, in near total isolation as minorities. In accounting, African-American representation had been so scant that they had called each other by number, recalled North Carolina A&T's Dean Craig, on hand as one of the Project founders. He had been Number Eight, he told the group.

Dean Craig also had a wisecrack—he thanked the PhD Project sponsors for the plentiful breakfast they had provided.

But, he quipped, he could not understand serving breakfast to that many African-Americans and not offering grits.

Sitting in the audience, Laura Hall smiled at the comment. But at the breakfast buffet the next morning, to her astonishment, a silver serving dish piled high with grits appeared. She was amazed, she would later explain, to have encountered an African-American man "powerful enough to have grits appear in Chicago!" Seeing people of color exert power in this setting—the power to create such an event, even the power to make grits appear—Hall began to understand why her dean had insisted she come.

Also taking a seat in the audience was Olenda Johnson, a third year doctoral student at the University of Pittsburgh. She too was there because of Dean Stith, her former professor and mentor. Until that moment, she had known only three other people of color—two of them in her school—pursuing doctorates in business. Just meeting others at the hotel "was a blessing in and of itself," she would later recall. "Even though we had loving support of family and friends, we all lacked a resonant support system that truly understood the scope and the depth of our challenges—and the psychological strain."

At another corner of the room sat Patricia Martinez, a Californian who had flown in with interest, but with no intent of actually entering a doctoral program.

The two days of the conference began to unfold. It had been put together with care and great thought all summer and fall by the planning group, which had had to invent it all: There was no guide on how to create such a conference. Remarkably, through two decades, the program agenda they devised would undergo virtually no substantive change. They had nailed it almost perfectly the first time.

After deans and doctoral program heads provided a detailed overview of the PhD cycle, Michael Clement led a lengthy session in which current doctoral students shared their experiences—often in personal detail. Later, a panel of faculty members told the audience about the ultimate prize—the life they could enjoy as professors. Among the panelists: Sandra Shelton, a lonely doctoral student no more. She was now Dr. Sandra Shelton, an accounting professor at DePaul University. Having taken the position, she had just officially finished her PhD at Wisconsin two days earlier.

The bulk of the afternoon was devoted to the university recruiting hall, where the 266 participants could learn more, tailored to their individual interests and concerns, by meeting directly with the 67 representatives of doctoral programs whom Dean Stith three months earlier had assured Milano would never show up.

The following morning was devoted to breakout sessions for each of the five major business disciplines. Olenda Johnson sat on the panel of management doctoral students, but preceding them was a panel of experienced management professors. "As each shared their experiences and the impact they had on their students, the tears for me just started flowing," she recalled. "I immediately felt in my heart a clarity of purpose and fuller understanding of my calling. I would be touching lives in more ways than I could imagine."

The information systems panel was led by Laura Hall, the struggling student who had been told by her professors not to even try.

A closing session tied it all together in an uplifting recap. The 266 participants had easily learned more, in these two days, than they could in months—if at all—on their own. Among the panelists in that finale was Dr. Shelton.

As preparations for that session took place, Milano turned to team member Tara Perino and said, "You know, Sandra just defended her dissertation and she's officially a PhD. We have to do something."

"I know," Perino replied. "What did you have in mind?"

Milano shrugged and walked off to attend to another matter.

Perino looked around her makeshift command post and saw a PhD Project display her team had created. Part of it was a prop, a mortarboard graduation cap with the organization's now instantly recognizable rainbow tassel affixed. She snatched it up and tucked it under her arm.

A short time later the final session concluded, lifting the room to an emotional pitch. Milano took the microphone for a surprise announcement: The PhD Project had already achieved its first graduate, he said, and there would now be a graduation ceremony. The crowd fell silent, uncertain how this could be possible.

Sandra Shelton was called to the podium, and the cap that Perino had picked from the display booth was placed atop Dr. Shelton's head to loud cheers and applause. The signature moment of every PhD Project conference since then—the capping ceremony—had been born in a burst of spontaneous, inspired improvisation.

To Olenda Johnson, sitting in the audience, "There was a sense of awe and immense pride, excitement and once again affirmation of the path God had me on."

Patricia Martinez, the Californian who had come to the conference largely from curiosity, had been greatly surprised to realize the depth of commitment needed to earn a doctorate, but equally impressed at the strength of the support system The PhD Project was promising to help people through it. By that morning, she had made the life-changing decision: she would become a professor. She had listened carefully to Dr. Shelton's talks and found her to be "a huge, vivid, personified example of what could be in store for me." Watching Dr. Shelton get "capped" served as a confirmation of the decision she had just reached.

Laura Hall had already experienced her emotional peak. Listening to Dean Stith, Milano and Dean Craig—the man who made grits appear—she had heard "things I had never heard before. How important I was, how much difference I could make, how much impact I could have, and all I had to do was keep on my path. These three men changed my life fundamentally just by believing in me, supporting me and contributing every resource they could drum up."

Of that first PhD Project cohort, 50 would go on to enter doctoral programs, and 33 would complete. Of these, 32 were still teaching in 2014. They are:

Dr. Tanya Benford, Dr. Paul Brown, Dr. Pamela Carter, Dr. Beatriz Rivera Cruz, Dr. Gail Dawson, Dr. Kimberly Ellis, Dr. Elisa Fredericks, Dr. Luis A. Garcia, Dr. Rosanna Garcia, Dr. Jorge Gonzalez, Dr. Kimberly Grantham, Dr. Joyce Jackson, Dr. Jo Yvette Lacy, Dr. Karl Lawrence, Dr. William Lewis, Dr. Leyland Lucas, Dr. Patricia Garcia Martinez, Dr. Karen McDougal, Dr. Sylnovie Merchant, Dr. Alisa Mosley, Dr. Karen Nunez, Dr. Harriette Bettis Outland, Dr. Susan Perkins, Dr. Vanessa Perry, Dr. Ronald Ramirez, Dr. Charles Richardson, Dr. Joe Ricks, Dr. Quinetta Roberson, Dr. Nolan Taylor, Dr. Karynne Turner, Dr. Michelle Williams, Dr. Satina Williams, Dr. Lynette Wood.

9

The 1994 conference was a high point, but just a beginning. At the onset, the planners had not known, until the first responses filtered in, whether there was demand for their offering. In 1995, as they expanded the outreach and launched a second campaign, they found that indeed there was: the second conference drew more people than the first, with 324 attendees. Since then attendance has ebbed and flowed only moderately, from a low of 290 to as many as 442, generally counter to the direction of the economy.

The PhD Project model, successful as it was in attracting and informing, still had two major gaps to close. To fulfill the promise made to Carolyn Callahan, student associations for all five business disciplines had to be created. Other sponsors would have to step forward to help fund all this. The Project began a proactive effort to attract new ones that continues to this day. All original four founding sponsors remain as contributors, now augmented by an impressive list of corporate and other sponsors. In addition, universities—both doctoral granting and non-doctoral granting—now participate and contribute financially.

With this support, the information systems student group started in 1996, with the other three launching in 1997. Each group has met every summer since then.

The second gap was actually an extension of the journey. Minorities are even more underrepresented at the leadership levels of higher education: deans, department chairs, provosts and other administrative positions. In 2010, The PhD Project introduced Project AHEAD to increase diversity at this level (See The Next Frontier: Moving AHEAD)

The milestones unfolded:

At the November 1998 conference, Dr. Alisa Mosley, the first attendee of the 1994 conference to complete her doctorate and thus become the first PhD Project professor, was duly capped at the closing session.

In 2002, Dr. Alisha Malloy became the 588th minority professor, doubling the number of minority business faculty since the Project's formation. She was nicknamed Dr. Double.

In 2005, The PhD Project was reorganized as a separate 501(c)(3) corporation, with KPMG continuing as lead sponsor and administrator. KPMG's total commitment as of publication date was $16,750,000.

In 2007, Dr. Belinda Shipps became Dr. Triple when she became the 882nd business professor.

In 2009, Dr. Shalei Simms became the 1,000th minority business professor in the U.S.

In 2011, The PhD Project created a Hall of Fame. The inaugural inductees: Dr. Quiester Craig, Dr. John Elliott, Bernie Milano, Dr. Mel Stith and Dr. Andy Policano.

In 2012, Dr. Miles Davis became the first PhD Project professor to be named a business school dean—at Shenandoah University. Dr. Carolyn Callahan, Dr. Ralph

68

Katerberg and Dr. Tom Lopez were inducted into the Hall of Fame.

In 2013, Dr. James Alvarez-Mourey became Dr. Quatro as he represented the quadrupling of minority business faculty since the Project's formation. Dr. David Ford, Dr. dt ogilvie and Dr. Mimi Stamps were inducted into the Hall of Fame.

In 2014, John Fernandes, retiring as president of AACSB and serving as chair of The PhD Project board of directors, observed, "I don't think the job is done, but certainly our 20 years of progress have been probably 40 years' worth."

Once the building blocks were in place, the PhD Project's participants carried it from there. They became PhD Project professors and, spreading across academia, fulfilled the vision of the founders. They became mentors, role models and advisors to countless undergraduate students, both minority and majority. They also helped each other: each new incoming doctoral student would be mentored, formally and informally, by a more senior student or a faculty member. As that student rose in seniority, he or she would reach out and mentor a newer student, all the while still benefitting from the continuing mentorship of those ahead of them. Many of these stories are documented in the chapters that follow.

As a critical mass of new professors developed, something else happened. As their numbers became more prevalent, PhD Project professors could tap into the group and find a research collaborator or resource for virtually any need. If it was for an introduction to a scholar in the field they did not know, perhaps for research or employment-seeking purposes, chances are that person was no more than one or two degrees of separation away through the PhD Project network. PhD Project professors were finding job opportunities, gaining entrée to present at prestigious conferences and publishing in important journals—on their own, with no direct involvement by the Project's administration—through relationships they developed thanks to the Project.

By the mid 2010s, there was still a long way to go: minority representation in the business disciplines was still far from where it needed to be. But the generation of professors The PhD Project created—the new face of business education—had taken on a life of its own.

10

Several factors may explain why The PhD Project succeeded despite the doubts of the supposed experts. First was the simple, in hindsight, recognition that the target audience was mid-career business professionals rather than recent graduates. Second was the decision to approach the diversity challenge as a marketing challenge needing a marketing solution.

The richness and completeness of the annual conference agenda was a critical factor. An event that tried simply to expand the warm and upbeat tone of the marketing would have failed. It would have excited all who came, but would not have explored and answered the doubts and questions they would have gone home with. The conference had to simultaneously sell the career choice of academia, openly examine the real challenges it posed and show possible paths to overcoming those challenges. This it has done, brilliantly, and continues to do each year.

Additionally, establishing the Doctoral Students Associations was critical to the high completion rate that Project participants achieve. Doctoral students consistently describe their summer DSA conference as an essential annual re-energizing experience. More than one has arrived at their meeting fully intending to announce they are quitting, only to be talked off the ledge by peers. Less dramatically, but more frequently, doctoral students not only learn what they will experience next on their journey, but meet the journal editors who will publish them and the faculty members who will collaborate with and work alongside them, for their entire career.

Much has been said over the years about the speed with which The PhD Project was put together: less than a year from formulation of the core idea to the first conference. The standard take is that businesspeople, being less consensus-driven, tend to move faster than academics. The full picture is more nuanced. The sheer enthusiasm and energy of the founding group and the excitement over creating something new and potentially significant propelled them forward and enabled them to disregard normal conventions and protocols. Additionally, Bob Elliott has noted, Bernie Milano's role within KPMG placed him on the boards and committees of practically every organization in the country that could help in any way in the creation of The PhD Project, and he utilized those connections to accelerate the process. "You put practically anybody else in that slot, and Michael Clement's estimate that it would take 10 years might even have been optimistic," Elliott says.

This leads to one more factor. "The PhD Project has a million fingerprints on it," Milano likes to say, and this is true. But it is also indisputable, as Elliott and every other person involved in the effort has readily said, that the driving force and guiding spirit of The PhD Project at every step has been one Bernard J. Milano.

Carolyn Callahan identified several characteristics that Milano brought to the table back in the early 1990s: "Bernie had the vision. He is, first of all, good at identifying what the issue is: How should we solve this problem? Who are the key people who can make it happen? How can I support them?"

"Bernie," she added, "is one of those people who can identify what you can do, long before you think you can do it."

Bob Elliott, in 2004, placed these characteristics in the context of Milano's career arc and The PhD Project's formation: "He foresaw a partial solution to a great national problem," Elliott noted, "at a time when Milano was eligible for retirement from the KPMG partnership.

"But he didn't retire; he entered into a mighty blaze of creativity, achievement and public service.

"Without Bernie, there would be no PhD Project, many fewer minority faculty members in American business schools and many fewer minority students with role models and mentors. Bernie is, quite simply, the soul of The PhD Project."

Dr. Theresa Hammond, whose research into diversity and accounting provided one of the original scholarly sparks for The PhD Project, looked back at all that has followed and said, "Everything lasts a few years and disappears. Then everybody's reinventing the wheel, acting like they're the first person with a program to diversify the profession. These seem to just come and go, and unfortunately, not a lot have a lasting impact.

"The PhD Project has had such a lasting impact. It will continue to have a lasting impact, because it is taking the long run approach of putting faculty in place who will make a difference for decades for their students. There's just nothing that makes me happier about what the profession has done than this."

The PhD Project conference continues to take place every year, at the same airport hotel, in November. The same electricity and excitement that Dean Stith experienced on that first night, and the same cheering, applause and tears that filled the room when Dr. Shelton was capped, still occur at every conference. Every summer, doctoral students gather at their respective Doctoral Students Association meetings to reenergize and make new connections that will sustain them through decades of mentorship, support and collaboration as they take their places in the academy and change the face of business education.

Michael Clement is now the Accounting Doctoral Program Director, KPMG Faculty Fellow in Accounting Education and Professor of Accounting at the University of Texas at Austin.

Theresa Hammond is now Professor of Accounting at San Francisco State University.

Carolyn Callahan is former dean, College of Business at the University of Louisville, and now Associate Provost and Brown-Forman Endowed Chair in Accounting there.

Sandra Shelton is now KPMG Distinguished Professor of Accountancy at DePaul University.

Peter Johnson, the happily non-doctoral instructor from Hawaii who accidentally bumped into the Accounting Doctoral Students Association crowd at the 1994 AAA conference, was motivated by the encounter to attend the following year's PhD Project conference. He is now Dr. Peter Johnson, Ernst and Young Fellow and Assistant Professor of Accounting at the University of Alabama, having been attracted there by PhD Project Professor Dr. Thomas Lopez.

Laura Hall is now Associate Professor, Information Systems, University of Texas at El Paso. She won the state's top teaching award for her exceptional work with undergraduates, and inspires every parent, single or married, with her story at every PhD Project conference.

Olenda Johnson is now Professor of Strategic Leadership and Leader Development at the College of Operational and Strategic Leadership, U.S. Naval War College.

Patricia Martinez is now Associate Professor with tenure at Loyola Marymount University.

Dean Craig retired in 2013 after 41 years as dean at North Carolina A&T. His farewell celebration spanned three days and attracted a thousand people. He stepped down having hired 15 PhD Project professors, mentored dozens more and inspired many of his own undergraduates to become professors. He serves to this day as a frequent source of insight for The PhD Project's leaders.

Peter Thorp and Bob Elliott similarly retired with honors and kudos from business.

Dean Stith became dean of the business school at Syracuse University.

Bernie Milano and Tara Perino continue to head the team that operates The PhD Project and the KPMG Foundation.

More than 40 graduates of the precursor MSI program, at first written off as a failure because its participants did not immediately enter doctoral programs, ultimately did— becoming professors through The PhD Project.

Leading the Way

Two Meetings

Dr. Mark Dawkins
Associate Dean for Academic Programs; Associate Professor of Accounting
University of Georgia

At a tense meeting one day in the early 1990s at a large, heavily white university, a student watched in silent respect and admiration as his mentor—a senior African-American faculty leader—stood up to academic ignorance and prejudice and stared it down. The student saw—perhaps for the first time—that it was possible for an African-American man to challenge the status quo and influence thinking within a predominantly majority culture. The moment crystallized into an indelible memory and life lesson for the student.

About a decade later at another well-known, mostly white university a few hundred miles away, a similar scenario unfolded. This event, too, would be long remembered as a learning moment by a young African-American man observing it.

Such experiences are probably more common in modern times than in the pre-diversity past. What makes this story special is the role that Dr. Mark Dawkins plays in the two events.

Actually, the *roles*:

In the first meeting, Mark Dawkins was the student watching his mentor in quiet awe. In the second, it was a different young man drawing inspiration as his mentor stood up for the needs of African-American students in the business school. That mentor was the very same Mark Dawkins—by now risen to become an associate dean.

Such is the nature of mentorship at the most meaningful level: it passes its lessons forward to future generations. This too is a fundamental goal—and increasingly a tangible outcome—of The PhD Project.

When the first meeting recounted in this story took place, Dr. Dawkins was a PhD candidate in accounting at Florida State University's College of Business. The college was already a nationally admired beacon of doctoral diversity because of the unceasing efforts to attract candidates of color by its dean, Dr. Melvin T. Stith. As his successes multiplied, majority faculty members pushed back: "You're lowering the standards by recruiting so many people of color," some claimed.

A meeting was called, and it grew heated. Then Dr. Stith stood up and presented the facts: minority students, as a group, had scored higher on the GMAT exam than the majority students admitted to the program. The opposition to greater diversity at the business school wilted.

This was so strong a memory for then-doctoral student Mark Dawkins that more than two decades later, unprompted and in detail, he would recall it vividly: "There was a lot of push-back from faculty, and Mel stood his ground. He showed them that their concerns were misplaced. No standards had been lowered. He deserves a lot of credit, in my book, for how forcefully he stood his ground and pushed for diversity at Florida State."

Doctoral student Dawkins became Assistant Professor of Accounting at the University of Georgia. Focused foremost on developing his research and teaching, he still found time to join efforts to attract African-Americans to his new academic home.

"I live in a state that is 30% African-American and about 14% Hispanic. At my university, African-Americans represent about 8%, and Hispanics about 5%," he says. "It is personally important for me to make sure that the university has diversity on our campus."

A few years after arriving at Georgia, Dr. Dawkins teamed with the state's C.P.A. society to win a $10,000 grant to create a summer program that would introduce minority high school students to the accounting profession and encourage them to pursue it in college. That first year, 1998, 10 high schoolers took part. From this modest start, the program has mushroomed into a four-day, on-campus "accounting camp" that draws 100 students, corporate sponsorship and guest lecturers from every major accounting firm. Every summer without fail, Dr. Dawkins shows up to meet and teach the young men and women who attend.

Through this and additional diversity recruitment programs that he participates in or oversees, several hundred minority high school students gain an up-close and in-person glimpse at the advantages of studying accounting at the University of Georgia. Up to 15% of them go on to study accounting there, and the vast majority of the others take up business studies at other colleges. Success has many parents, and Dr. Dawkins does not claim credit, but diversity at the business school significantly exceeds that of the university overall.

Dr. Dawkins achieved a professional milestone in 2008 when he stepped up to become associate dean for Academic Programs at the business school. "We need to have more people of color not only in the front of the classroom, but also making decisions about the priorities of the university and the direction that it takes," he explains. "You can't make those decisions unless you're seated at the table. As professors we have direct impact on students through teaching, but in administration you have a broader impact on the university."

The seed for his decision to enter administration had been planted many years earlier. The long-term role model for Dr. Dawkins was none other than Dean Stith. Often, Dr. Stith had told him of the joys he experienced upon meeting the happy parents of a graduating student on Commencement Day. At one such session, he told the soon-to-be Dr. Dawkins: "This is a pretty good experience. It's something you should consider."

As Associate Dean, Dr. Dawkins has a full spectrum of responsibilities that span all aspects of the academic program. Among them in 2014 were the development, from scratch, and implementation of an entirely online new Bachelor of Business Administration degree program; creation of a functioning private equity fund for alumni to fund and invest with input from undergraduates; and planning for a future entrepreneurship center within the school.

Just as junior professor Mark Dawkins found time to focus on his passion for increasing diversity, so does

Associate Dean Dawkins. A role model and mentor to countless students, he continues to interact with minority admissions prospects at the "summer camps" and with undergraduates through such roles as faculty adviser to the campus chapter of the National Association of Black Accountants (NABA). It was in this capacity in the mid-2000s that he met and began mentoring an African-American young man with aspirations of a successful career in accounting.

High school senior Bryan Davis knew, from his first visit to tour the University of Georgia, that he wanted to major in accounting. After meeting Mark Dawkins that day and hearing from him about the university's accounting program and research opportunities, he decided this was where he would become the first in his family to attend college.

Certain of his career goal but far less confident in his capacity to succeed in a majority-dominant college and work environment, the young man arrived on campus and thought, "There is literally no one here who looks like me." (Outside of Dr. Dawkins, that was clearly the case in the accounting department.) "No one I can look up to and say, 'Oh, that's how you do it.' No one who can say, 'This is how you interact and communicate your skill set in an organization that doesn't have people who look like you.'"

Why this was so, and why it mattered, he would explain years later, is because "Culture makes a difference. Others may not have the same perspective as you about leadership, about having confidence in a room full of people who don't look like you."

Just by going about his daily business, Dr. Dawkins changed the young man's life:

"I would see him walk into any room at the university and be as comfortable as if he was in his own house," Davis recalls. "He would just walk up to anyone and talk to them. He wouldn't stutter. He wouldn't sweat. No nervousness.

"That," Davis says, "was the biggest inspiration I ever had. Otherwise, I would not have thought that I could be successful like that."

Active in the NABA chapter, Davis attended the meeting recounted at the beginning of this chapter. Unlike the heated session a decade earlier in which Dr. Dawkins was the student, the issue here was not a charge of lowered academic standards, but one of sheer ignorance as to why minority students needed their own organization when the college already had one for all accounting students.

Listening as Dr. Dawkins calmly and methodically (and ultimately successfully) explained the rationale for funding the NABA group, the young man experienced the same revelations and emotions as doctoral student Dawkins had many years ago, on the day Melvin Stith stood his ground and systematically decimated the claim that increased diversity was decreasing academic quality. And, like Dr. Dawkins before him, Davis would be able to easily recollect vivid details of the moment many years later.

Demonstrating the confidence and poise he developed as an undergraduate mentee of Dr. Dawkins (the skill set was never in doubt), Bryan Davis sought and won a prestigious internship at the U.S. Financial Accounting Standards Board—a competitively fought-for position seen in the profession as a powerful career-launcher. Today, he is a technical accounting advisor, focusing on financial instruments, derivatives and hedge accounting in the treasury department of GE Capital, the nation's eighth largest financial services company.

Special Issue

Dr. Geraldine Henderson
Chair, Marketing Department
Rutgers University

Dr. Jerome Williams
Distinguished Professor and Prudential Chair, Marketing
Rutgers University

The May 2013 arrival of the American Marketing Association's *Journal of Public Policy and Marketing* in business professors' mailboxes was a watershed moment. It signaled the maturing of diversity in business as a recognized, even essential field of academic study. This had not been so prior to the existence of The PhD Project.

At first glance, that May 2013 issue looked like all the others before it. But this was the JPPM's Special Issue on Marketplace Diversity and Inclusion, the first time the prestigious journal had devoted an entire issue to the topic.

It was also a watershed moment for The PhD Project: of the issue's 17 articles, all but four were authored or co-authored by PhD Project professors. In all, work by 20 scholars affiliated with the Project appeared in its pages.

That special issue was conceived, driven and edited by two veteran faculty members who had, since Day One, influenced the Project and countless of its students and professors: Drs. Geraldine Henderson and Jerome Williams.

"It is no longer a viable strategy for companies to stick their collective 'heads in the sand,'" they wrote in their introduction to the issue. "Instead, private and public sectors should enact policies to ensure active interest in and respect for diverse marketplaces throughout the globe."

It is easy to see why marketers are increasingly interested in diversity: the consumer world they serve is an increasingly diverse population in a global marketplace. But the academic community has not historically shared this interest. Now, largely as a result of The PhD Project's existence, the body of diversity-related academic research is growing exponentially in marketing and also expanding in the other academic disciplines of business: management, accounting, finance and information systems.

Dr. Williams and several other pioneers were early and strong originators of diversity research in marketing even before The PhD Project formed in 1994. But that year marks the start of The Project's story, and it is also the year when Geraldine Rosa Henderson enters the scene.

She enters it in top form. Walking into the inaugural PhD Project conference that December, she is completing her doctoral studies at a Top 25 business school, Northwestern, and has already accepted a professorship at another Top 25, Duke. She is an instant "poster child," role model and mentor for the first class of PhD Project participants.

And when she settles in at Duke the next fall, she excels, instantly.

"Against all odds, she won teaching awards the first time she taught. *Nobody* does that," recalls PhD Project professor Dr. Tiffany Barnett White, then a Duke doctoral student. "People who have written reams of books can't do that. She was superlative."

On track to go far. the prestige of a top university attached to her name, but in a few years' time... she says goodbye to Duke and moves on.

Colleagues who don't know her well are at first perplexed. But to those who know her better or who look closer, the move to Howard University in Washington, DC is logical, sensible, perhaps even inevitable. For the leadership at Howard has recently announced intent to elevate its research focus—in precisely in the same areas where Dr. Henderson has come to realize that her deepest interests lie: compelling issues relating to marketplace diversity and multiculturalism in marketing.

And this—especially back in the 1990s—is not considered mainstream material, neither in content nor methodology. It is not what junior faculty members at top drawer research universities are encouraged or rewarded to do. Each time Dr. Henderson publishes a paper on a diversity topic, she hears someone say, "You know, you really need to get back to the main focus of your work."

But, she decides, this is the main focus of her work. And so she packs.

"That," Dr. White reflects some 15 years later, "took a lot of courage. She was doing the thing she was expected to do, and doing it quite well. But she wanted to do research that had meaning, and for her that was in marketplace diversity."

"It was a personal decision," Dr. Henderson recalls today. "I needed to make a change, a radical change."

The academic community's sparse enthusiasm for multicultural research could not be fully explained as an expression of prejudice, ignorance or elitism. The prevailing paradigm Dr. Henderson and others were challenging had a conceptual aspect: mainstream marketing research held that consumers should be studied as one complete entity, encompassing all groups, for consistent, accurate theory to emerge. Only in this way, it was said, could universal rules and truths emerge. Drs. Williams and Henderson and other pioneers said, in effect, "No; we can learn more by studying the differences than we can by ignoring or dismissing them." Dr. Henderson's move to Howard said that loudly.

From there on, including turns at the University of Texas and now at Rutgers University, Dr. Henderson would speak loudly by publishing prodigiously—often with Dr. Williams but also with other scholars within and without The PhD Project:

"Responses to Consumer Discrimination"
"Consumer Empowerment in Multicultural Marketplaces"
"Social Justice in a Global Marketplace"
"Consumer Racial Profiling"
"Born a Suspect: Shopping While Black"
"Encouraging Urban Entrepreneurship"...

The papers would pour forth abundantly. The full list runs many pages. Interspersed with these would be an equal number of papers and presentations on what her profession's establishment would consider "mainstream" topics.

And as her curriculum vita expands, a new generation of minority doctoral students and professors, rising up through The PhD Project, takes notice.

They read her work in the journals, and at PhD Project conferences, they meet her in person. Role modeling, mentoring and collaborations ensue: Dr. Henderson actively seeks out such opportunities because, she has discovered, mentoring and role modeling are also passions that fill her with energy and purpose.

Perhaps the first African-American doctoral student to be deeply influenced by meeting Dr. Henderson was Dr. White, who is now associate professor of marketing at the University of Illinois. She believes that the impact of the professors who pioneered diversity research reaches far beyond their mentoring of PhD Project participants.

Early in The PhD Project's life, Dr. White—who was there at the beginning and has herself mentored as many doctoral students as anyone—observed that some minorities considering the career switch to academia would eventually retreat: their attraction was based on an interest in exploring diversity-related research, and in those early days they discovered what Dr. Henderson once had: that this wasn't the path to mainstream success in academia.

"Gerri, Dr. Williams and Dr. Sonya Grier legitimized the field by publishing on these research questions in the best journals," says Dr. White. "They are opening doors for other scholars, and they are opening the eyes of potential scholars."

As The PhD Project enters its third decade, Dr. White sees fewer prospects turning away from academia for fear that exploring diversity will go unrewarded. She sees more minority doctoral students pursuing such research.

Dr. Kevin Thomas is one living example. His story illustrates the strong hold of the prevailing wisdom that has long marginalized diversity research.

Drawn to the enticing prospect of trading his corporate job for the life of a business professor, Kevin Thomas came home from the 2005 PhD Project with high hopes, excitement and confidence. All of which were soon dashed: he applied to seven schools and received seven rejections.

Evaluating the outcome with as much objectivity as he could muster, he was nonetheless puzzled: on paper, he seemed a solid candidate. Thinking, "There's something about this I'm missing," he reached out for advice from professors he had met at The PhD Project and in his earlier MBA studies. Gradually, a realization emerged: he'd been expressing a hunger to pursue diversity issues in his research, and mainstream academia was not enthused.

Something else emerged from those discussions: "I kept hearing the name of Jerome Williams at the University of Texas," Dr. Thomas recalls. "I finally gathered the nerve to email him, and then to call him for advice."

For the first time, the aspiring academic found himself talking to a respected scholar at a leading institution who shared his passion. The two men clicked almost instantaneously.

Jerome Williams, notwithstanding a 10-year career in business and a pre-tenure focus on mainstream research topics, had known since high school that he would one day want to study issues relating to diversity and discrimination. While in fourth grade, his family had moved from heavily minority center city Philadelphia to an integrated suburban community nearby where school officials promptly, without testing him or notifying his parents, placed him in special education. The decision was reversed, but even at that age young Jerome knew that an injustice had been done. Just a few years later, he would watch with combined disbelief, pride and concern as news media crews descended on his pleasant Northern-state suburban block: the African-American lady three doors down from him had just bought a home in an adjoining all-white community, Levittown, and it was national news.

By 1994 when The PhD Project started, Dr. Williams had earned his PhD, begun climbing up the academic ladder and was finally turning his attention to research in areas relating to diversity. This direction, he recalls, "was not always respected and accepted." Well intending mentors and advocates encouraged him to follow the mainstream so as to advance his career. By the time Kevin Thomas found him, Dr. Williams had succeeded in pursuing his passion and earning national recognition for his scholarship.

Although Austin, Texas was among the last places where Southern Californian Kevin Thomas expected to live, he applied to enter the University of Texas doctoral program and study with Dr. Williams. The application was accepted.

Even under Dr. Williams' wing, the long reach of mainstream academia's prevailing wisdom continued to pull forcefully at the doctoral student. He selected for his dissertation a safe, data-driven retail-marketing topic, relegating his passion and scant free time to a side project exploring the depiction of African-American men in magazine advertising. Before the doctoral student got to finish his dissertation, Dr. Williams accepted a position at Rutgers and left Austin. Kevin Thomas was momentarily without an on-campus mentor.

One day he shared his side interest with another marketing professor he had met at Austin, Geraldine Henderson, who had moved there after Howard. She found it "really interesting."

Dr. Henderson started paying closer attention to the young PhD candidate's work, and one day she asked, "Why isn't that your dissertation?"

"Would they let me?" the student asked.

Assured that the department would, he then asked her, "Who would I get to chair my dissertation committee?"

The answer to that question, of course, was standing right in front of him. Dr. Henderson calls the dissertation on millennial African-American males that resulted from this exchange "very fascinating work" that examines the question of whether the United States is in a "post-racial" era.

"Kevin's work is going to transform consumer research," she predicts.

Dr. Thomas, now an assistant professor at the University of Texas, is already a prolific and published researcher—on the topics that continue to intrigue him.

Summing up the state of multicultural and diversity related research in business academia in 2014, Dr. Williams says, "Doors have opened up, but it's not yet where it should be."

Dr. Henderson joined Dr. Williams at Rutgers, where she now chairs the Marketing Department.

She, Dr. Williams and Dr. Thomas collaborate and co-author papers on issues of diversity and consumers.

Mentor of Mentors

Dr. Carolyn Callahan
Associate Provost, Brown-Forman Endowed Chair in Accounting
University of Louisville

Dr. Carolyn Callahan, former Dean of the College of Business at the University of Louisville, and former KPMG Distinguished Professor of Accounting and Director of the School of Accountancy at the University of Memphis, was the first African-American woman to earn tenure in accounting at a doctoral-granting university.

One of the active participants in The PhD Project's formation, she was also one of the first African-American women to head a major university's accounting program and has been a member of an important federal government financial advisory board as well as a respected teacher and researcher. Dr. Callahan is perhaps most talked about for an enduring change she has driven: improving the education and preparation of doctoral students and junior faculty.

Born in poverty to a factory worker and a domestic, Dr. Callahan went on to success in college and then in corporate accounting. Ultimately, she heard and answered an inner calling: to pursue an academic career. Upon realizing that it would take a PhD to fully realize her dream she hesitated, unsure if she could meet the rigorous challenge. She reached out to seek the opinions of her favorite undergraduate professors. They told her, "We know of no African-American woman who has ever earned a doctoral degree in accounting." But they also assured her that if she chose this path, they had no doubt that she would achieve her goal.

Dr. Callahan has written that nothing she had experienced in life to that point prepared her for the degree of prejudice she encountered in the upper reaches of academia she now entered.

"I was absolutely stunned by the accepted training of a doctoral student and totally unprepared for the emotional toll of the complex problems facing the few African-American women in academe," she later wrote in a published anthology.

What she encountered was more than ordinary racial prejudice: "Although I met all intellectual challenges required by the rigors of my doctoral program, I found the accepted training of a doctoral student unduly intellectually restrictive and at times very demeaning. The isolation and loneliness were debilitating."

Determined to overcome the challenges of earning a PhD and the rigors of junior faculty status, she did—with distinction. But her doctoral experiences gave birth to ideas that would drive the career that followed: the newly-capped Dr. Callahan vowed to create a different experience for the countless doctoral students and tenure-track young faculty who would follow and study under her: "I decided to interact with my doctoral students in an entirely different manner, to treat them as my colleagues and to invite them to be full co-authors on my research projects."

While still untenured, she gave full co-authorship credit to a graduate assistant, who by tradition would have been merely thanked in a footnote. She did so despite pressure from senior faculty to conform to norms: "I said I didn't care; it felt right for me," she later explained.

She also concluded that the very fundamentals of the doctoral process were seriously flawed: an "apprenticeship model" in which students are "entirely dependent upon the goodwill of tenured professors who are not subject to any accountability." That too, she decided, would have to change. This decision would define her career as she proceeded to earn tenure—twice—and then turn her beliefs into practice in positions of increasing prominence and responsibility from the 1980s on, at Massachusetts, Notre Dame, the University of Arkansas, at Memphis and, as of 2013, Louisville.

Arriving at Arkansas in 2001 as director of the accounting doctoral program, she brought with her a mission—and won university backing of it—to restructure the traditional apprenticeship model she so disliked. The model she created would hold tenured professors accountable and required weekly meetings with doctoral students, joint research teams with assistant professors participating and full co-authorship credits for students. Not that PhD candidates would be coddled under the Callahan model: they were expected to complete their studies in three to four years, hopefully having presented or published in a top-level forum.

In her tenure, the Arkansas doctoral program attracted higher-quality students, increased its funding by 50% and won recognition for national publications and presentations. The

University of Arkansas honored the Callahan model with its Provost's Award.

Influenced and mentored often by veteran faculty members—many of them white males—in her early academic days, Dr. Callahan made an entry in her mental "accounts payable" ledger. As an established professor, she began taking on the mentor role herself, almost without noticing: "I think I'm that way about most things in my life. If I can be helpful, I want to be. It's just who I am as a human being. If somebody is walking out off the curb, I'm probably the person that's going to jump up and try to pull them back."

Metaphorically, Dr. Callahan has yanked many a doctoral student and junior faculty member back to the safety of the curb and helped guide countless more advance down their path. One of them is now Dr. Gregory Ramsey, assistant professor of Information Systems at Morgan State University. He recalls the day he "hit a snag" nearing completion of his doctorate. It was more like a sinkhole: having already left the college of his PhD program in Minnesota for a fellowship in New York, he was told that he needed to rewrite his doctoral dissertation. He had no clue what to do next. The PhD Project connected him with Dr. Callahan, who was in Memphis. She took him on "as one of her own students," and coached him through the crisis despite the geographical and cross-discipline challenges, he recalls. "She's like Superwoman, flying around in a cape with an "S" on her chest helping doctoral students," says Dr. Ramsey.

In the mid-1990s, newly named assistant professor of accounting Sandra Shelton received her first invitation to present a scholarly paper. "*I need some mentoring,*" she told herself. She drove from Chicago to meet with Dr. Callahan, whom she had met at an early PhD Project planning meeting, at the University of Notre Dame in South Bend, Indiana. By the time she returned home, Dr. Shelton knew exactly how to deliver the presentation. So began a friendship and mentoring relationship now into its third decade. Paying it forward, Dr. Shelton has gone on to mentor innumerable doctoral students, both within The PhD Project and through all her other work. In 2010, an exceptionally promising undergraduate in her class revealed an interest in pursuing an accounting doctorate. Dr. Shelton pointed the young woman, Porschia Nkanska, in the direction of Memphis where Dr. Callahan then chaired the School of Accountancy. Quietly and behind the scenes, Dr. Shelton encouraged her mentor to admit her mentee to the doctoral program. Ms. Nkanska excelled when she arrived, and with a recommendation and support from Dr. Callahan, received a prestigious internship in Washington, DC at the Public Company Accounting Oversight Board. Upon completing her degree and starting what appears to be a very promising career, she will be a third direct link in a chain of mentorship that traces back to that 1994 meeting in Montvale, NJ.

And so, says Dr. Shelton, Carolyn Callahan is "a mentor of mentors."

Dr. Shelton is now KPMG Distinguished Professor of Accounting, a title also once held by Dr. Callahan, at DePaul University.

"I have developed a deep empathy for the vulnerable in the academy because I personally know the pain of being an 'outsider' inside the university. I view an academic career as a life of service to one's students, colleagues and profession.

When I go into the classroom, I feel a moral obligation to challenge my students on an intellectual level. Faculty popularity contests and grade inflation, with its associated ills, do not serve our students well. I am often told that minority students need me as a role model; however, I feel that my majority students also benefit from my presence. I try to stress the importance of ignoring physical attributes in assessing competency. I embrace the responsibilities of the trailblazer and I hope other women and minorities will follow my path."

Excerpted from Labors From the Heart: Mission and Ministry in a Catholic University, University of Notre Dame Press, 1997.

A Secret Mover of the Needle

Dr. Jorge Pérez
Professor of Information Systems
Kennesaw State University

Tenured professor Dr. Jorge Pérez didn't fully appreciate his decision to branch into senior administration at Kennesaw State University until one morning several months into his term on the university Cabinet, reporting directly to the president. Around 11:00 that day, he proposed a major new initiative to the president.

By 2 P.M. the president had assembled the provost and several vice presidents and deans to discuss the idea. By late afternoon, the plan had been launched toward becoming a reality on the suburban Atlanta campus of 25,000 students.

"A very large initiative that has changed the institution pretty significantly was born that day. That's intoxicating to me—the ability to watch my ideas take flight," says Dr. Pérez. Increasingly, PhD Project professors—many of whom held senior, influential positions in business before entering academia—are advancing to college leadership roles. They are discovering that while the joys of being a professor and influencing a few dozen or few hundred students are indeed great, the opportunity to leave one's mark over a wider footprint affecting tens of thousands can be irresistible. They are also discovering that prior experience as an executive or manager prepares them to excel at the skill sets required of a dean or department chair (as of mid-2014, approximately 52 PhD Project professors had stepped up to fill an administrator's chair).

Dr. Jorge Pérez arrived at Kennesaw State as an assistant professor of Information Systems in 1998. The event almost never happened at all.

Two years earlier, gainfully employed as a non-doctoral instructor, but drifting without motivation to complete his dissertation, he had packed uncertainly for the first-ever meeting of The PhD Project's Information Systems Doctoral Students Association in 1996.

Also attending that meeting was a man he had not seen in some time: the chair of his dissertation committee. That encounter, and the excited buzz emanating from the other doctoral students, renewed his spark. He spent several hours talking with his dissertation chair and made a momentous decision: to leave his teaching job and return to the PhD program to complete his doctorate. "Had it not been for that meeting," he now says, "I might never have pulled the goal back within reach."

At Kennesaw, and finally titled Dr. Pérez, he rapidly emerged as a gifted professor. Focusing at first—

appropriately, for a new assistant professor—on the building blocks of attaining tenure (reached in 2004, after just six years) and promotion, he soon found his interest turning to university-wide matters beyond his department. It was the early 2000s, a period when the professional class in America was adjusting to the rise of the technology-based workplace. As an information systems expert, Jorge Pérez understood this strange new world far better than most of the humanities, social sciences and marketing academics populating the campus. Named a Faculty Fellow for E-Learning, he soon acquired a reputation as Kennesaw's "tech guru." Excelling in this new role, he co-created and taught two courses in computer literacy—one for the students, another for the faculty.

His reputation grew, and in 2009 he was offered a coveted position: a three-year term on the university's Cabinet as the Faculty Executive Assistant to the President. It was in this role that he delivered the morning pitch for an idea that became a done deal by day's end.

"Until then, information systems was my field. When I took that appointment, leadership became my field," he recalls.

Engaged in overseeing the daily operations of a major public university, he found the experience to be "the most intensive job I've ever had; incredibly challenging. I learned how difficult and nuanced leadership is," he explains. "Celebrating people for what they accomplish, and at the same time challenging them to continue to grow, is incredibly difficult. I observed the president and his senior cabinet members on a daily basis trying to do their best at a very difficult thing.

"It changed me fundamentally. It catalyzed in me a very deep interest in exploring my own leadership abilities. Leadership is a calling, and I hear the call."

When the three-year term ended, the president of Kennesaw State proposed a wager to Dr. Pérez, who was by tradition expected to return to his original faculty job: "I'll bet that if you do, you'll be back in my office within six months telling me that you're pursuing another leadership position."

The president was correct—Dr. Pérez had indeed been changed profoundly and permanently by his exposure to leadership. But there was a third alternative, and it was the one Dr. Pérez chose.

The American Council on Education (ACE) awards approximately 50 prestigious Fellowships annually that prepare promising faculty members and administrators for senior leadership roles in academia. Dr. Pérez applied for and was awarded an ACE Fellowship for 2013-14.

ACE Fellows work for a year at another institution under the direction of top administrators. Dr. Pérez selected the Massachusetts Department of Higher Education for his fellowship placement. Working on strategic planning with the senior deputy commissioner for academic affairs of that state's 29-campus public higher education system, he became engaged with education policy on a statewide level. The experience, which required him to work with local campuses on implementing a central system vision, heightened his desire to continue growing as a leader: "The complex interplay of how institutions in a system relate to the state, the legislature and each other is very fascinating to me.

"In the broadest sense, the biggest benefit of the fellowship is learning—very intensive learning about leadership. I also learned about myself, and that will help me have a better sense of what trajectory I want to pursue next."

As to that Kennesaw State initiative that Dr. Pérez proposed at 11 A.M. and saw launched three hours later: he chooses not to disclose what it was. Barely anyone other than the university president ever knew that he was the idea's originator.

"And that is OK," he explains. "One of the most lasting lessons of leadership is that it doesn't matter who gets the credit, as long as the needle moves."

On campuses across the country, the needle is starting to move in ways large and small, visibly obvious and subtly long term, as PhD Project professors like Dr. Pérez begin to make an impact on higher education policy.

2013-14 was a banner year for The PhD Project and ACE Fellowships. Three of the six business professors selected as ACE Fellows that year were PhD Project professors. The others were Dr. José Antonio Rosa of the University of Wyoming and Dr. Charles Wesley Richardson, Jr. of Clark Atlanta University (see: Road Less Traveled).

Changing the Face of Business Education

Four Directions

Dr. Joseph Gladstone
Assistant Professor, Public Health Administration
New Mexico State University

Dr. Deanna M. Kennedy
Assistant Professor, Management
University of Washington Bothell

Dr. Amy Klemm Verbos
Assistant Professor, Management
Central Michigan University

Dr. Daniel Stewart
Associate Professor, Management
Gonzaga University

L ong ago, Native Americans were clever and proficient entrepreneurs. Interacting with European trappers and traders, they engaged successfully in businesses of many kinds with the new arrivals.

And then everything changed.

In modern America, few Native Americans—living on the reservation or in the mainstream—study business or pursue management careers. Even fewer teach business.

One reason is that western business revolves around such values as competition, maximizing profit and short-term outcomes. Native businesses often focus on different concerns: How can my business benefit my community? How can I compete with my rivals in a way that lets us all survive? For many, studying business is not "the Indian way."

This dichotomy helps explain why Native Americans are, by far, the most underrepresented minority in U.S. business schools at a time of pressing need in Indian Country for skilled managers to run community businesses and medical and social service organizations. The growth and increasing sophistication of tribal businesses in gaming and other industries heightens the need for business-savvy talent. But when Native Americans look at business schools, they see no one who looks like or thinks like them. And so they look elsewhere for a career path.

Four Native American business professors, who met through The PhD Project, aim to address this challenge. They have embarked on what they expect to be a career-long effort to inject Native ways and thinking into classroom materials, activities and curriculum. Their goal is far-reaching and game-changing: to greatly increase the ranks of Native Americans majoring in and teaching business.

"We want to see management education that doesn't clash with Native values," explains one of the four, Dr. Deanna Kennedy. "How do we communicate to students that it's okay to create a business and be respectful of others, to maximize your profits and best benefit your family? How do we communicate that management education doesn't have to take away your Native identity? We want to think about how we can make management education more accessible and also more interesting."

It was an atypically balmy week before Thanksgiving 2003 in Chicago, but Joseph Gladstone, just off a plane from Arizona, had little concern for the weather. He was about to attend The PhD Project annual conference—to decide if he was ready to switch careers, and add one to the tiny number of Native American business professors in the U.S.—himself.

A tribal public health program manager in Indian Country, Gladstone had long noted—and fretted over—the dearth of management talent within the organizations that served his community. He had observed how this deficit adversely affected his people. He had found himself wondering, "Is it my calling to do something about this?" In the soul-searching that ensued, an answer crystallized one day: "I can do more good for Indian Country as a business professor than I can by managing one tribe's health division."

The very next day, Gladstone pulled from his mailbox the latest issue of one of the few magazines targeting educated Native professionals. The first page he flipped to contained an ad that asked the question, "Have You Thought About Being A Business Professor?"

His immediate reaction: "Wow! Yes—just yesterday!"

That ad was Joe Gladstone's introduction to The PhD Project. The amazing timing of its arrival was like a thunderbolt: *"Yes, this is a calling."*

Now, two years later and ready to make the career switch, Gladstone arrived at the conference with a suitcase full of apprehensions: *The invitation said "business attire" and I don't own a suit. Will I see anyone who looks like me? Can I do this?*

Then came the session where newly minted management professor Dr. Daniel Stewart took a seat on the panel. *A Native American: someone who looks and thinks like me— and shares my academic interests,* Gladstone thought. At that moment (a moment at which there were 15 Native American professors in U.S. business schools) Joe Gladstone realized that if he could achieve his dream of becoming a business professor, he wouldn't be alone.

Within a year, Gladstone was enrolled in the management doctoral program at New Mexico State University. Attending his first PhD Project Doctoral Students Association (DSA) conference in Atlanta that summer, he received further confirmation, in the form of two other Native American DSA participants—PhD candidates Deanna Kennedy and Amy Klemm Verbos—that he wasn't alone. Naturally, the threesome began talking about their lives and their studies.

They talked animatedly during session breaks, after hours and before hours. Not only had Gladstone found two peers, he quickly discovered that both shared his passionate concern for the dearth of Native American undergraduates studying business. The discussions turned to those concerns and continued via e-mail through the academic year. They resumed and intensified at the following summer's DSA meeting.

By the third summer, as the Management DSA gathered in Anaheim, it was time to move beyond talk. "Why don't we do something about this together?" Gladstone asked his two friends as they chatted one day over coffee.

The "something" that emerged was audaciously sweeping in scope: if traditional management education's content and style clash with Native culture and turn off Native students, why not reinvent them? Why not develop a new kind of management education, harmonious with Native values? It was an idea so vast and challenging that only a concerted, long-term effort by a dedicated group could hope to accomplish it. And that is exactly what the three Native American doctoral students began to set in motion that day in Anaheim, adding strength by drawing in Gladstone's original inspiration, Dr. Stewart.

Still in its early years, this effort includes collaborative research (they have published or presented several papers already), workshops for educators, presentations at academic conferences and community outreach. Working in shifting combinations on different projects, and sometimes singly with their universities, the four hope to redefine business education for Indian Country's would-be entrepreneurs and managers of casinos, hotels, tourism services, social service agencies and community businesses. "If the classroom is conducive to learning what and how Native Americans want to learn," says Dr. Kennedy, "then we may attract more Native American students to our classes while enriching the learning experience for everybody."

"To practice business does not go against the Indian way. Trading is in our blood," adds Dr. Gladstone. "The idea of business not being Indian is a recent belief in our history, since the reservation era. Our native trading spirit has been taken away from us."

Storytelling, for example, is integral to Native culture. Dr. Verbos is taking the lead in holding workshops for other educators on weaving storytelling techniques into the classroom curriculum: "This is the kind of creative, inductive learning approach to teaching management education topics that we think needs to be introduced," she explains. She and her colleagues have published or presented several papers on the topic, including in the prestigious *Journal of Management Education*.

Much of the work to be done in building Native capacity to run businesses lies off-campus. Not every Native American manager has—or will—attend college. So Dr. Kennedy is helping to lead an initiative by her university to bring management education to tribal communities. The University of Washington Bothell's tribal leadership business program covers key business areas—budgeting and accounting, team leadership and project management—and overlays it with mentorships. The program will be delivered at multiple locations to reach all of Washington's tribes.

"One of the most salient issues seems to be knowledge transfer within and between tribes," Dr. Kennedy says. "How to start businesses? How to create economic growth on the reservations? What has worked? What hasn't?"

This foursome forms a powerful synergy, because they bring complementary skills to the table. Dr. Kennedy is an expert in operations. Dr. Verbos brings Native American perspectives and values into management education. Dr. Gladstone studies the intersection of American Indian culture and western management philosophies. Dr. Stewart's area is entrepreneurship. In a culture where the focus is often on local and tribal ventures, entrepreneurship is a highly needed skill. "In order for Native Americans to stand on their two feet economically, individual entrepreneurship is going to have to be key," Dr. Stewart says.

Combined, their four areas of expertise align with a central concept in American Indian beliefs: that of the Four Directions (East, South, West and North): "Everything in Indian Country operates in the four directions," Dr. Gladstone says. "That fits with the four of us, because all of those different strategies are needed for Indian Country to develop itself economically."

Four directions and a road that is potentially endless. "We see this as long-term research," says Dr. Kennedy. "One of the great things about being a professor is that you get to pretty much dictate how you want your life to go. You have the freedom to look into what you really want to. And we see the process of making more Native American professors as long term."

"When I'm done and I look back on it," adds Dr. Verbos, "I'd like to see Indian Country having very savvy business people—people who can protect the business interests of their communities."

It is too early to measure results from this ambitious but still emerging work. But two things are certain: first, there would be no fruit from this collaboration—there would be no collaboration—without The PhD Project. "None of this would have happened without the PhD Project," says Dr. Verbos in an assessment her peers share. "I've met colleagues I never would have met. The Project has been responsible for my most productive stream of research."

Adds Dr. Gladstone, "We would not have known we existed. The PhD Project was the hub that brought us together."

Second, there is cause for hope: the number of business graduates from Native American tribal colleges rose 39% from 2003 to 2010, according to the American Indian Higher Education Consortium.

If the past is any guide, many in this new generation of business students, and those to follow, will one day knock on the doors of a Native professors like Drs. Gladstone, Kennedy, Stewart and Verbos. They will—perhaps tentatively at first—seek out advice on finding a job or doing better in class. Or ask for a letter of recommendation.

It will happen because the professors profiled here, and all Native American professors, send a silent message. "For Native Americans to complete a Bachelor's degree is an accomplishment," says Dr. Gladstone. "Moving on to earn a PhD is an even greater achievement. So I serve as a role model for Native Americans in business—and for earning an advanced degree and going back to the community, serving it as an educated person."

It is happening already, and with increasing frequency, and it is why The PhD Project was created. "I think the purpose of the Project, to place academic role models within the classroom, is becoming reality," Dr. Gladstone says.

"Tough Love"

Dr. Thomas Lopez
Ross-Culverhouse Endowed Chair of Accountancy
University of Alabama

The first-year PhD candidate, an African student with five small children under age six, was struggling greatly with the intense rigors of adjusting to doctoral study. His doctoral committee, meeting privately to review the unpromising record before it, gingerly turned its discussion to talk of the exit door.

"Maybe," one faculty member said reluctantly, "it is time to acknowledge that we made a mistake." Dr. Thomas Lopez, another member of the committee, leaned forward and said firmly, "No. I think he can do it."

The committee ultimately agreed to let the student continue, but Tom Lopez knew he had just added another project to his plate: helping this student right his path and advance to a successful academic career.

It would not be an unfamiliar mission for Dr. Lopez, a longtime PhD Project participant and mentor. He has mentored so many, for so long and so well, at every level of accounting education nationwide, that he was among the first non-founders admitted to The PhD Project's Hall of Fame.

In this case, Dr. Lopez knew the struggling student not only on campus, but through The PhD Project. He had reached the critical conclusion that prompted him to speak out in the young man's defense: this student had the talent to succeed. But Dr. Lopez also knew the student faced an exceptional personal challenge: adjusting to a new country with a young family. So the veteran professor sat down with the fledgling scholar for a pep talk. It ended with the same words countless others had heard Dr. Lopez speak: "If I could do it, you can do it."

As a motivational technique, this phrase is among the more frequently used tools in the standard coaching and mentoring toolkit. But numerous PhD Project doctoral students and junior faculty report that the message resonates with uncommon clarity and force when delivered by Dr. Lopez.

The reason lies in who Tom Lopez is, or more precisely, who he was. First stop on his career journey was Miami, a city he served for 13 years as a police officer. Next came seven years as a C.P.A. Only then did he turn his sights toward academe and earning a PhD. Clearly, this is a person whose professional roots are wrenchingly real-world and non-abstract. Today, Dr. Lopez is—as a third career—a widely respected, oft-published scholar who holds the Ross-Culverhouse Endowed Chair of Accountancy at the

University of Alabama. He is a highly regarded, deeply committed academic who comes across as a regular guy. Because he is. And so, when recounts his life story and says, "If I could do it…," struggling doctoral students listen.

But to the doctoral student with five young kids at home, that phrase was just an opening parry. Over months that turned into years, Dr. Lopez met regularly with the student. The meetings were often tough, and the message was blunt. Harsh words, the kind not usually associated with the rarefied halls of academia, sometimes flew in both directions. When it was all over, four arduous years later, the student graduated at the top of his class.

Today, the student needs just two words to recall and characterize those sessions: "Tough love," says Dr. Nelson Alino, who is now Assistant Professor of Accounting at Quinnipiac University.

"There were times when I wanted to quit," he remembers. "Tom would tell me, 'You have five kids. You need to teach them not to quit, so show them that you aren't a quitter.' That gave me the encouragement I needed to continue and finish.

"He would push me to the limits sometimes, and when he saw me starting to break, he knew the right words to bring me back. Without him, it would have been a different story for me."

Although Nelson Alino was one of many he has mentored over three decades, Dr. Lopez recalls the experience well: "What I saw in Nelson was a person with a lot of talent, but having a tough time expressing that talent and finding the right area to work in. And, with five kids and a wife who wasn't working, he literally couldn't afford to fail. He needed somebody to be hard on him, to help him."

And the coup de grace: "I was looking at a man who came through the PhD Project. There was no way I was going to let him fail. There was no way. He was going to have to fight me."

"There were times I regretted things I said to him. Words can be like bullets—they hurt. I know I said things that hurt him. But I could see the other side of it: here's a guy who has what it takes to be successful; he just needs somebody to help encourage him, get him over the hump. Did I feel bad about some of the things I said to him? Yes. Do I still regret it? Not a bit, not a single bit. Because look at him now."

Dr. Juan Manuel Sanchez, another PhD Project professor who met Dr. Lopez through the organization, saw another side to the "No Quitting" mindset surface when he and a third PhD Project professor collaborated with Dr. Lopez on a research paper. The prestigious journal reviewing it raised one vexing challenge after another with each successive draft. The effort faltered; its wheels began wobbling. Two of the three co-authors were frustrated enough to consider waving the white flag. The third was Tom Lopez. "We're going to plow through it," he told his partners. They did, with Dr. Lopez taking the lead in resolving issues with the editor. The journal published the paper in 2011.

Collaboration is a hallmark of Dr. Lopez's research work. At the 1999 PhD Project conference, a young prospective doctoral student searched in vain at the university recruiting fair for a professor at Arizona State University he had heard might be a potential mentor. The man was nowhere to be found, but at another university's booth, Craig Sisneros encountered a newly minted professor who had just completed his doctorate at Arizona State. Tom Lopez, there to recruit doctoral students for the school that now employed him, earnestly plunged into a lively discussion on the attributes of Arizona State. The young man, sold, enrolled there the following year and developed a strong friendship with Dr. Lopez that blossomed into a professional collaboration. Dr. Lopez and Dr. Craig Sisneros, now Assistant Professor of Accounting at the University of Colorado Denver, have published two papers in leading journals together and are working on more.

Dr. Sisneros, nominating Dr. Lopez to the PhD Project Hall of Fame in 2012, noted that Dr. Lopez has attended every single PhD Project conference since presenting at the first one as a doctoral student. In addition, he said, Dr. Lopez has formally and informally mentored an endless stream of doctoral students through the Project's Doctoral Students Association: "Tom's constant presence and positive attitude at the annual conference has been an inspiration to countless numbers of prospective students that are now in their programs or have finished and are now on faculty."

Beyond his engagement with The PhD Project, Professor Lopez has long been an active advocate for diversity in a number of other educational settings. Among them: serving on the President's Minority Affairs Review Committee while on faculty at the University of South Carolina and for two years on the AICPA's Minority Initiatives Committee. At Texas A&M, his first faculty position, Dr. Lopez developed and led a business careers awareness program, designed to increase minority undergraduate enrollment at that college. After moving to the University of South Carolina, he developed a similar program there. Both programs are still operating successfully today.

Dr. Lopez, asked how as an active professor and researcher he found time to mentor undergraduate and doctoral students replied, "That's what I get paid for, that's my job." Actually, it isn't. Universities pay their faculty to research, publish, teach and serve the institution. The rest is, at best, optional. Tom Lopez respectfully sees it differently: "It seems part of the makeup of an accounting professor is to do some mentoring and try to help people get somewhere. I feel it's my responsibility to try to help as much as I can. I've helped some high school students on getting into college accounting or finance programs. I've helped some undergraduates who were struggling in their programs to become successful, graduate and start into careers.

"When students say 'Thank you for helping me, for providing time, for seeing me,' they don't really need to. Because really, seriously, that's my job. To help them be successful."

Mentorship: Pass It Along

Dr. Miriam Stamps
Associate Professor and Chair Emeritus, Marketing Department
University of South Florida

Dr. Carolyn Massiah
Professor of Marketing
University of Central Florida

When a young Miriam "Mimi" Stamps was still of an age when maternal influence is real and present, her mother advised her to become a teacher.

The future Dr. Stamps promptly rejected that advice. It was a time when women were first beginning to think beyond the pre-feminist era stereotypes that had limited their career choices. Some years later, as her husband pursued a career in academia, an opportunity for Mrs. Stamps to teach at the college level materialized. This was a challenge she welcomed and accepted. To her great satisfaction, she realized that "this was very different" from what her mother had envisioned for her. She also came to realize, quickly, that she would be the only minority faculty member wherever in academia she looked.

It was the beginning of a long and significant career as a professor of marketing for Dr. Stamps, who rose to become Chair of the Marketing Department of the University of South Florida. Along the way, she developed and sharpened an acute sense of the importance of reaching out to young students needing career and life guidance. "I fell in love with teaching and with the impact a teacher could have on students' lives," she recalls. When The PhD Project was formed in 1994, she embraced the opportunity to mentor and help develop a new generation of scholars from minority backgrounds.

"You don't just teach," she explains, "you preach."

Dr. Stamps' role as a mentor and life coach grew so great that she was inducted into The PhD Project Hall of Fame.

Among the many to have been touched by Dr. Stamps is Dr. Carolyn Massiah, now a marketing professor at the University of Central Florida. After hearing Dr. Stamps speak at the last session of the last day of her initial PhD Project conference, she introduced herself. An e-mail and phone mentoring relationship began almost immediately; Dr. Stamps advised and guided the would-be scholar, first on applying to and selecting a doctoral program, and then through all the hurdles, exhilaration and trials of earning the degree. Rising up the ranks as a successful doctoral student and junior faculty, Dr. Massiah continued to rely on sage advice and mentoring from Dr. Stamps. When her turn came to get prepared by veteran PhD Project professors for her first job interviews, Dr. Stamps was assigned to coach her. "It was a phenomenal, complete circle for that to happen," Dr. Massiah recalls.

Once she had reached the first rungs of success, Dr. Massiah asked her mentor how she could pay her back. The answer, at first, surprised her.

"She said, 'it's not about paying me,'" Dr. Massiah recalls. "She said there was a young lady she wanted me to talk to and guide."

The "young lady" was Rebeca Perren, a prospective doctoral student who was trying to decide whether to become a business professor. Dr. Stamps had encouraged her to attend the annual conference of The PhD Project to guide her decision.

Just as Dr. Massiah had connected with Dr. Stamps at her first PhD Project conference, she now assumed the identical role for Ms. Perren. She became a full-fledged long-term mentor to the prospective academic, who would shortly be accepted as a doctoral student at Dr. Massiah's university. The bond developed quickly and tightly: "By the next summer," Ms. Perren says, "we were doing research together."

Dr. Massiah went on to co-chair Ms. Perren's dissertation committee. A strong new link was forged in the chain of mentorship that started when Dr. Massiah first met Mimi Stamps.

Dr. Stamps also continues to mentor Ms. Perren, who says, "I'm not special—it's more like the rule. I know many students who have gotten critical advice from her."

"You have to reach back and help others make it," says Dr. Stamps. "When I look at The PhD Project, I see person after person do that. For me, that's what it's all about." Dr. Massiah, in her still unfolding academic career, continues to view Dr. Stamps as "a lifeline if I need it." Meanwhile she has leapt at the opportunity to mentor and guide undergraduates, even bringing one young research assistant to attend the 2013 PhD Project conference.

That student, Carlos Robles, switched his major from communications to marketing after taking Dr. Massiah's course at the University of Central Florida. "It's such a different experience having a minority professor, because you make not just an academic connection but a human connection," he said at the PhD Project meeting. "I feel I am not a student at a huge university, but an individual with the potential to become something greater."

Whether or not Robles ever becomes a professor, Dr. Massiah believes that every time she touches the life of a student, "I am helping to pay back everything The PhD Project has given me."

Changing the Face of Business Research

Fulbright Scholar

Dr. Renée Pratt
Assistant Professor, Management Information Systems
Washington and Lee University

The trail to one of the first Fulbright Scholarships awarded to a PhD Project participant* traces back to Toronto, Canada and the 2008 meeting of the Project's Information Systems Doctoral Students Association, and leads to a lecture hall at Germany's famed University of Potsdam.

"Renée, when are we going to write our first paper together?" Dr. Randy Bradley, one of that DSA's most popular and engaged mentor-professors asked newly-minted PhD and friend Renée Pratt at the 2008 conference.

As a first year professor, Dr. Pratt was gratified to receive this unsolicited invitation from a widely published, more senior faculty member. Her instant reply boldly stepped over those inner feelings. "How about now?" she suggested.

Dr. Bradley accepted, and a research collaboration was born.

For Dr. Bradley, it was one of many such arrangements: his hallmark, as a senior doctoral student and then faculty member (see An Unusual Promise) was collaborating with other PhD Project scholars. For Dr. Pratt, it was an invitation that would lead her research in directions she had not anticipated.

The two scholars were hardly strangers, having met at Dr. Pratt's first DSA meeting in 2003. By the following year, she was secretary of the organization, and Dr. Bradley, as immediate past president, was coaching her as well as being her cohort on leading the group. A year later, he was encouraging her to run for top leadership of the DSA—which she did.

So it was not a complete surprise for Dr. Bradley to suggest to Dr. Pratt in 2008 that they collaborate. Nor was it unexpected for her to see how readily her focus on business enterprise systems melded with his concentration in health care enterprise architecture. What she didn't anticipate was her rapidly increasing fascination with health care issues. She and Dr. Bradley would collaborate on four papers over the next two years. Before long, the two were interviewing hospital administrators across the United States on the emerging issue of electronic health care record systems—or, in the tech-talk of Dr. Pratt's discipline, "post-adoption diffusion of technology."

Specifically, Dr. Pratt became intrigued at the technological aspects of the burgeoning business, medical and public policy issues surrounding the inexorable spread of electronic medical record keeping systems. So deeply did she dive into this vital topic that, in a very short time, she was well published, well versed and developing a reputation for expertise in it.

Receiving a Fulbright Scholarship in 2012 to pursue this research further in Germany was high-level validation of the quality of her scholarship. A Fulbright is one of the most competitive and prestigious awards programs for research in the world. A Fulbright award appears on the resumes of more Nobel Prize laureates than any other honors program: 53 Fulbrights have received Nobels; another 78 won Pulitzer Prizes.

Dr. Pratt, whose mother was a nurse, spent much of the 2012-13 academic year in Germany. There, she studied that country's move toward electronic health record systems and what lessons the United States might learn from the German experience. Near the end of Dr. Pratt's research stint, Dr. Bradley was invited to co-present a symposium at the University of Potsdam with her. Scholars and practitioners at the German university listened carefully as the two PhD Project professors offered their insights on international opportunities and challenges in the health care information systems field.

The questions arising within her area of interest are compelling ones that affect every American: how can hospitals and providers better use electronic health recordkeeping to enhance operational and clinical outcomes? To reduce medical errors? To control costs? What is the appropriate balance between maintaining security, patient privacy and centralized recordkeeping? These are questions that inflame passions in public policy debates. At the nucleus of them lie technology issues that can be explored dispassionately and analytically by management information systems scholars like Dr. Pratt.

Much rides on the governmental, medical and business decisions that will emerge in coming years, all of it influenced by the research that Dr. Pratt and others in her field are now conducting. None of these compelling questions is theoretical or abstract: under current U.S. law, the first stage of nationwide implementation of electronic health records is mandated for 2015 throughout the United States. Dr. Pratt's work in Germany has already produced two papers, with more on the way, as well as a teaching case based on her findings. She is now expanding her work to examine progress and conditions in the health care systems of other European Union countries.

Dr. Pratt is certain in ascribing cause and effect: "Had it not been for The PhD Project," she says, "I would not be where I am now. The people and the discussions through the Doctoral Students Association helped provide strength, awareness and support as I wove through the passage of the PhD and now the tenure process."

Dr. Pratt has since paid that forward: she served a three-year term as faculty adviser to a more recent cohort of IS doctoral students in The PhD Project's DSA.

"Doctoral students call me all year long," she says. "They want to know, 'What's it like to go through the job interview process?' 'What's it like to be a minority in a majority-dominant school?' 'How do I balance research, teaching and service?'"

Some of these doctoral students summon the courage to ask her, or Dr. Bradley, if they can collaborate on a research paper together. She considers each request with the memory of the day in 2008 when Dr. Bradley invited her to co-author with him.

"My door, my phone—everything—is always open when those questions come in," says Dr. Pratt.

"I have an opportunity to mentor students of all groups and hopefully provide them insight and preparation for our diverse workplace," she has said. "It is my hope that my experiences in the workplace—private and public—and in academics, will encourage, motivate and engage others to explore computer systems and information systems in ways they never imagined."

Dr. José Rosa, a two-time Fulbright recipient and active faculty participant in the PhD Project, earned his PhD before the Project's inception. PhD Project professors Dorothea La "Chon" Abraham received a Fulbright in 2008, and Dr. Efosa C. Idemudia received a Fulbright in 2014. Also in 2014, PhD Project professor Dr. Stephanie Yates was chosen by the prestigious Fulbright Specialist Program to participate in a travel abroad project in Cape Town, South Africa.

Influencing Research Nationally

Dr. Quinetta Roberson
Professor of Management
Villanova University

Sitting in the crowded meeting hall among 265 other hand-selected participants at the first PhD Project conference in December 1994 was a soon-to-be former financial analyst and small business development consultant from Philadelphia. Quinetta Roberson would go on to become one of the first PhD Project participants to make the successful leap to academia, and within a decade became the first professor of color to attain tenure at Cornell University's School of Industrial and Labor Relations.

Not content to rest on tenured laurels, Dr. Roberson eventually moved on to Villanova University. In her research too, she was prone to carve out new directions rather than follow well-beaten paths. A leading scholar of organizational behavior, she acquired a reputation for her exploration of fair treatment at work and how management of diversity can improve organizational effectiveness. "I'm always into doing stuff that no one else has done," she likes to say, half-jokingly.

In 2012-13, an opportunity that played right to those core traits developed. A one-year directorship opened at the prestigious National Science Foundation (NSF). "I thought, here's a chance to have an impact," she recalls.

At NSF, as Program Director for the Science of Organizations (SoO), her role was to make funding decisions about research projects submitted by scholars nationwide. In applying new criteria to the decision-making, Dr. Roberson influenced the course of research in organizational behavior on a national level.

While many PhD Project professors do important research that advances their disciplines, Dr. Roberson in her NSF role had a broader, more interdisciplinary impact than any individual researcher ever could. Funding the kind of cutting edge work she believes is critical to America's global competitiveness, she supported projects that will widen and deepen the academic knowledge base that American business needs. She also created funding opportunities for scholars not accustomed to receiving NSF grants, including underrepresented minorities.

With a $4 million budget for Dr. Roberson's program at NSF, the SoO division is one of the nation's leading funders of organizational research. Surprisingly, it is among the better kept secrets in academia; the line outside its door for grants is not as long as one might expect. Dr. Roberson worked to change that. "There was an urban legend that NSF didn't really fund management research," she explains. Also, many scholars believed NSF funding was too small and short-lived to justify the work of obtaining it. But once inside the organization and "seeing the secret sauce," as she puts it, she concluded that both assumptions were false. She broadcast the word widely through academia, especially in circles that hadn't traditionally tapped into the NSF funding source. Among them: PhD Project professors and other groups of underrepresented researchers.

Dr. Roberson was the first actively researching management scholar in many years to hold the NSF position. She brought to the role all the values, priorities and interests that made her a respected, innovative professor. In her own research, Dr. Roberson had long felt driven toward transformative issues at the forefront of her field. To no one's surprise, she used her $4 million NSF budget toward— and sought out—the same kind of work.

One project she backed will show energy companies how to improve power delivery by focusing on their systems and people as well as their hardware. Another will have a similar effect on engineering firms. Usually, engineering enterprises try to improve their effectiveness by studying research on engineering processes. Dr. Roberson supported research that would help them do the same by examining their *human* processes. She also awarded grants that will accelerate the study of virtual organizations. Another grant funded under her stewardship is exploring how teachers and principals can deliver better educational services through improved teamwork. True to her own passion for the cross-discipline approach, Dr. Roberson also collaborated with other NSF units to jointly support proposals that spilled across traditional academic borders.

Another of her goals, she recalls, was "to try to diversify the pool" of funding recipients. One of those people was PhD

Project professor Dr. Jeffrey Robinson of Rutgers University. After learning of the opportunity through Dr. Roberson, he obtained funding to convene a cutting-edge panel in Newark, NJ. The subject: academic research that might lead to new public policies for strengthening social entrepreneurship.

To non-academics, faculty diversity is often defined as the representation of people of color who stand up front in the classroom. But that is only one part of the picture. The real heart of academia is conducting and publishing research—the development of new knowledge. What most of the public, including many undergraduates, don't see is how the work of knowledge creation takes place away from the classroom. The paucity of diversity so evident in front of the business classroom is less visible, but equally or even more so pronounced, inside the academy's research-making machinery. Journal editors, review panels and senior faculty in this world are overwhelmingly white, and often from elite institutions.

Things changed within the SoO during Dr. Roberson's year at its helm as she trained her attention here. Dr. Roberson focused her attention to diversify this machinery within the SoO program.

"I made it a point to diversify the reviewer pools," she says. "I selected scholars from smaller schools, schools with a balanced focus on research and teaching and HBCUs. I sent messages out to the PhD Project list and other networks."

As a scholar of the subject, she did so with a clear purpose: "We know generally that diversity of thought produces a better outcome. I wanted to use that broad brush because it brings a more comprehensive perspective."

The research proposals that Dr. Roberson supported in 2013 will take several years to take form, get published and influence the business and academic communities. Still, it is not too early to assess the impact of her time at NSF. One of the agency's senior leaders, Jeryl Mumpower, offers this:

"NSF depends on distinguished scholars like Professor Roberson to take time out from their own research and teaching careers to work for the Foundation to ensure that the very best research on the science of organizations is supported. During her time at NSF Professor Roberson did just that, and she did it superbly. Her exemplary stewardship of the SoO program promoted the growth and advancement of a critically important field of social and organizational science."

The Diner Dishes

Rebeca Perren
Doctoral Student
University of Central Florida

Cinthia Satornino
Doctoral Student
Florida State University

Research is the raison d'être and lifeblood of the academic firmament's upper strata, where doctoral candidates and professors reside. Undergraduates, it has been said, absorb and process knowledge and MBA students apply it—but PhDs. create it. One important outcome of The PhD Project has been the development of a generation of minority professors contributing increasingly to the body of knowledge that fuels management education and influences the business world. PhD Project professors—and even doctoral students— have published in their fields' most prestigious journals and presented at the leading conferences.

But this doesn't begin to explain The PhD Project's emerging influence on academic research. Some professors affiliated with The PhD Project have consciously chosen to pursue areas of research that address core issues of diversity and minority participation in business. In all five management disciplines—accounting, finance, information systems, management and marketing—they are exploring new research topics, addressing the roles of minorities in business as practitioners and consumers that mainstream majority scholars have little touched. These are new realms of knowledge that the business sector, with its increased focus on issues of diversity in today's global economy, and the academic community hunger for.

An unexpected outcome of The PhD Project has been its role as an incubator for emerging and veteran scholars to meet, exchange and explore ideas and develop streams of collaborative research. These scholars not only might not have ever connected with each other were it not for the Project; they might never have even entered academia. Some of this research has already emerged. (See Four Directions; many other pairs and teams, too numerous to include here, are collaborating successfully and getting published.)

Much more collaborative research is developing. Here, the story of a pair of young scholars whose research collaboration began when they were randomly assigned as hotel roommates at a PhD Project conference:

Rebeca Perren, the doctoral student whose link in the mentorship chain (see Mentorship: Pass It Along) began when she met Dr. Carolyn Massiah at her initial PhD Project conference, made another meaningful connection at her first Marketing Doctoral Students Association meeting in 2010.

Waiting in line to register, she struck up a conversation with another woman at the counter. Before either could reach the front of the queue, they had discovered much in common: both were balancing a professional career with raising small children and each was about to leave a good job in the business world to launch a new academic career. Their interests, personalities and thinking meshed so closely that they stepped aside to let others register ahead of them, chatting intently for 30 minutes. Upon finally collecting their registration materials, Ms. Perren and her new friend, Cinthia Satornino, discovered to their disbelief that they had been randomly assigned as roommates.

"We kept on talking—we didn't stop talking for six days. Up until three in the morning some nights," Ms. Perren recalls. The two new scholars, about to enter their first year of doctoral study, left the meeting fast friends.

In their first two years—the coursework part of a doctoral program—both women, independently, developed a burning research idea they felt couldn't wait. With mutual encouragement and support, each jumped the starter's gun and dove in. Amazingly, they discovered their scholarly interests were also aligned—adding research goals to the list of things they had in common. When the next summer's Doctoral Students Association meeting came around, the talk reached deeper. Joining with a third doctoral student, Stephanie Lawson, they assembled after conference hours at a diner around the corner from the San Francisco hotel for a serious session of plotting out research avenues to explore together. None of the three had any idea where the session might go. "We snuck off to the diner to dish about our ideas," is how Ms. Satornino recalls their expectations.

What ultimately emerged from that lengthy brainstorming session, and others that followed, was a multipart research stream, already developing, that will stretch onward for several years. The women affectionately call their collection of ideas, papers, presentations and plans "The Diner Dishes." In all, they anticipate it will include at least seven pieces of research. Two have already been presented at academic conferences, one is scheduled for journal publication, several were reserved for Ms. Perren's dissertation and some are in development. Collaborating in different combinations, they are studying how consumers interact with each other in the marketplace.

"So what started as a wonderful, supportive relationship has grown," says Ms. Perren. "It's now a very productive research relationship as well."

Across disciplines and in another part of the country, accounting doctoral students Norma Montague and Nicole McCoy also met at their Doctoral Students Association meeting and became roommates. Like their sisters in marketing, this pair discovered a common research interest: in this case, examining and understanding the professional skepticism that public accountants bring to the independent audits they conduct.

This common bond made for interesting conversation at the summer meetings, but it wasn't until they had both completed their degrees and become professors that a concrete plan for joint research took root. They anticipate producing at least two academic papers from ideas they have already discussed.

Many other PhD Project-launched research pairs, triads and teams have formed across the five disciplines of management education, some of them discussed in other chapters here. Many of these scholars say they would have never entered the professorate had it not been for the Project. Most say they would never have even met their research partner had it not been for The Project.

Some, like the women in these stories, can trace their professional bonds back to the reservations systems that linked them as roommates at a PhD Project conference.

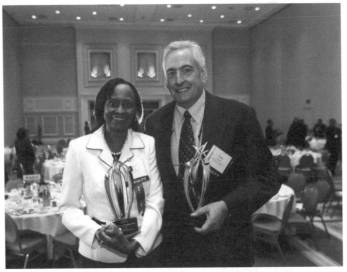

Dr. Carolyn Callahan and Dr. Tom Lopez with their
2012 Hall of Fame Awards

Dr. Miriam Stamps with doctoral student Rebeca Perren

Dr. Jorge Pérez   Dr. Dan Stewart

Dr. Adriane Randolph wearing Google Glass at the
Information Systems Doctoral Students Association Meeting

Dr. Angélica Gutiérrez

Dr. Quinetta Roberson

Bernie Milano with Dr. Michael Clement

Dr. Joe Gladstone

Dr. Mark Dawkins

Dr. Carolyn Massiah

Dr. Geraldine Henderson (far left) and Dr. Jerome Williams (right) with doctoral student Tyrha Lindsey

Dr. Randy Bradley and Dr. Martin Dias

Dr. Renée Pratt with H. John Hair, KPMG (left) and
Dr. Randy Bradley (right)

Dr. Amy Klemm Verbos and Dr. Deanna Kennedy

Dr. Charles Richardson

Dr. Ian Williamson

Dr. Stephanie Lawson and
doctoral student Cinthia
Satornino

Dr. Laura Hall

Dr. Miles Davis with Dr. dt ogilvie

Dr. Tiffany White

2011 Hall of Fame Inductees, (from l-r) Dean Melvin T. Stith, Dean Quiester Craig, Bernie Milano, Dean John A. Elliott, and Dean Andrew Policano

2012 Hall of Fame (from l-r) Bernie Milano (2011), Dr. Thomas Lopez, Dr. Ralph Katerberg and Dean Quiester Craig (2011)

2013 Hall of Fame (from l-r) Dr. Miriam Stamps,
Dr. David Ford and Dr. dt ogilvie

Dr. Joe Ricks (left) and Dr. Vanessa Perry (right) with a fellow
participant at the first PhD Project conference, December 1994

First Accounting Doctoral Students Association, 1994

First Information Systems Doctoral Students Association, 1996

First Marketing Doctoral Students Association, 1997

First Finance Doctoral Students Association, 1997

First Management Doctoral Students Association, 1997

Founders at the first annual PhD Project Conference: (l-r) Peter Thorp, Citigroup, Julie Dolan, GMAC, Bernie Milano, KPMG Foundation and Dean Mel Stith

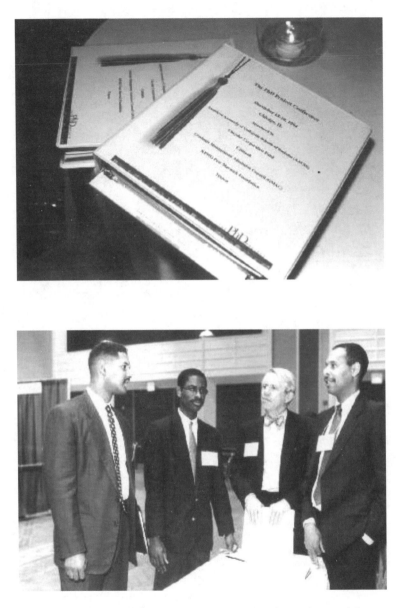

Dr. Michael Clement (far right) and Peter Thorp (second from right) talk with participants at the first annual PhD Project Conference

The PhD Project Annual Conference

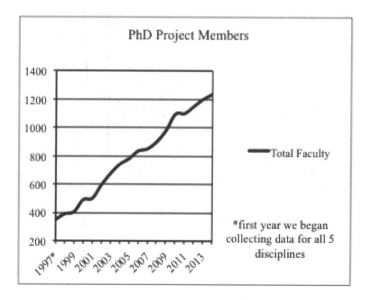

The number of diverse business faculty members has steadily
increased since The PhD Project began

Influencing Undergraduates

An Unusual Promise

Dr. Randy Bradley
Assistant Professor, Information Systems and Supply Chain
Management
University of Tennessee

It is a challenging extra-curricular assignment that the University of Tennessee hands Professor Randy Bradley on Saturday mornings each spring.

He is asked to stand up and face a room full of anxious high school seniors from underrepresented minority groups, most with uncertain parents at their side. These teenagers, many of whom will be first generation college students, are among the talented young people who have been offered admission to the University of Tennessee to study business. They have been invited on campus for an overnight visit to introduce them to life at the university. The event includes opportunities to meet and speak with faculty and students. For many students and parents, one thought hovers silently in the air as they stroll past neo-Gothic academic buildings, walking toward the business school: *How will a minority undergraduate fare in a majority-dominant institution of such imposing nature?*

Ultimately it is up to each student, and the university, to answer that question. Tennessee has made diversity a significant priority—as evidenced by the role it asks Dr. Bradley to play. But the first hurdle takes place at the reception for these prospects, most of whom have other attractive options for their college education.

Dr. Bradley, who is also an ordained minister, has done this Saturday morning speech before, and he knows what many in his audience are thinking: *"This man is the only African-American on a faculty of 130. He must have been brought up in an environment of privilege."* So he rises and tells them, "I lived in the projects. I understand what it is like to grow up in difficult circumstances."

Ensured of their attention, he looks each parent directly in the eye as he delivers an extraordinary promise:

"When you release your children to the university, you will be releasing them to me. As a faculty member and a mentor, I will interact with them daily or weekly.

"I will treat them the way you would treat them. And I will challenge them the way you would want them to be challenged. So when they come back to you, they will be better students and better human beings."

What makes the promise extraordinary is that Dr. Bradley finds a way to keep it. With open office doors and an open heart, he devotes significant chunks of time throughout the academic year to do what he told the parents he would do. Even the doors to his home open up. African-American business majors can usually expect to receive an invitation each year from Dr. and Mrs. Bradley to join them for one end-of-year dinner or cookout: around Thanksgiving, Christmas or Easter. Some years, the Bradley home overflows with upwards of 50 young guests, filling every available room and the back yard as well.

Another exceptional aspect of Dr. Bradley's promise is that, while also teaching and doing research, he does not limit his mentoring to undergraduates. If hitting three is a trifecta and hitting four is a grand slam, there is no word for what and whom Dr. Bradley reaches each year. He mentors or collaborates with those on all six rungs on the scholastic ladder: elementary, high school, undergraduate, graduate, doctoral and faculty.

As the only African-American on the business school faculty (at press time), Dr. Bradley cannot avoid being a role model. He does not merely accept the role; he cherishes it and extends it. The reasons reside in his roots and in his convictions: "When students come to me struggling and having challenges, I can relate because that is the life I once lived. And when I share my story with them, they recognize that if I did it, so can they."

The visible presence of a Black man in front of the classroom alters the perceptions of many majority students he teaches, Dr. Bradley adds. Some of them have never had a Black teacher at any point in their education.

And so holiday dinners at the Bradleys are even more than opportunities to break bread and build rapport with homesick students needing a mentor. Assessing what they have seen of him on campus and in the classroom, and now experiencing his generous spirit on a more personal level, many say as they depart, "You've inspired me to keep moving forward, because one day I want to be in a position to give back—as you have given back to us."

The inspiration and encouragement take a different form when Dr. Bradley steps off campus to face another challenging assignment: explaining the principles of supply chain management to local elementary school students, some as young as third grade.

This is neither a fool's mission nor an interaction with precocious 10-year-old business geniuses. It is, rather, his role in a university-community program to excite and entice schoolchildren in underserved communities to study business one day.

The children do not grasp business theory, but they do like sports. Dr. Bradley often begins by asking them to imagine it's their job to get their beloved Tennessee Titans football team out West for a road game. "How are we going to get the players and the coaches there? What about the equipment? What happens to the families?" he asks. Ideas and lively discussion then typically fly around the classroom, and when all issues have been explored he tells them, "You just talked about logistics and transportation management. You covered operations management. And you discussed the value of supply chain management in today's economy. We've been talking about what you learn when you study business."

The seeds planted in these visits, which Dr. Bradley does periodically, will be long in gestating. The horizon is medium-range when, in another program on campus, he meets with select high school seniors at a summer boot camp that aims to attract them to study business, preferably at the University of Tennessee. One of his roles has been to lead them through a visit with a regional accounting firm that sponsors The PhD Project, Dixon Hughes Goodman. The low representation of African-Americans in accounting has been widely documented and is a source of great concern to the profession.

"It is amazing to see how many students walk away from the experience at least considering accounting as a viable profession," he says. "It's so important because many students, especially from underrepresented groups, say the reason they don't choose accounting is because they don't know what it is. They may have never interacted with an accounting professional. In their mind, it's someone who works at a bank."

At the upper reaches of the academic progression, doctoral prospects and students—and even junior faculty members—find mentorship and inspiration in Dr. Bradley just as do undergraduates and high school students. One of them was 2005 PhD Project conference attendee Martin Dias.

A successful IT professional in banking earning a six-figure salary, Dias was the father of four girls under age eight the year he received two mailers about The PhD Project. These facts comprised the "Don't rock the boat" side of his mental ledger as he entertained the notion of becoming a professor. On the other side of the ledger was the excitement of pursuing new challenges and the opportunity to make a greater impact on others.

Thus conflicted, Dias attended the conference. His imbalanced mental ledger fell into place when Randy Bradley took the stage and told his story. "Here I see someone who looks like me," Dias recalls. "He has a family like me. He is active in the ministry like me. He is focused and determined like me. He's acknowledging this will be a challenge, but he's saying the end result will be worth it."

"He basically took all my excuses away."

With that, Dias went home to tell his wife he had experienced a life-changing moment. After much prayer and consideration, the family decision was made to move forward.

Following two years of preparation and planning, Dias resigned his corporate position and entered a doctoral program at Bentley University.

Seeing a young woman approach his office and request a moment with him momentarily startled Randy Bradley. This particular student wasn't one who participated heavily in class. She had not previously sought his mentorship, nor was she in danger of failing. What she said next was even more unexpected to him...

It wasn't hearing that the student was pregnant and torn by the painful decisions she now faced that surprised Dr. Bradley: life, he well knew, does not unfold for most people in a tidy procession of happy and planned occasions. It was that she had come to him for advice, even before facing her parents.

The student saw her choices as stark. Some of them, she realized, would hurt people who loved her. Most of them, she told Dr. Bradley, would mean dropping out of school.

For the tangled swirl of moral, religious and personal issues in her situation, Dr. Bradley could help her think them through, but he was not about to judge, recommend or encourage. On the issue of school, however, he stood firm. This young woman was a first-generation college student, he knew, and he was quite sure that she would never return to the university if she left. "However you ultimately decide to resolve your situation," he told her, "it would be a great mistake to drop out and never achieve all the things you have worked so hard to accomplish."

The student took that advice and, after making the personal decisions she had to face, returned to her studies. She completed her degree.

Of the freshman class prospects whom Dr. Bradley addresses each spring, he estimates that 50 to 75% end up accepting the admissions offer. University-wide, the acceptance rate for all entering freshmen is below 50%.

The then IT professional whose life changed when Dr. Bradley spoke at the 2005 conference is now Dr. Martin Dias, Assistant Professor of Management Information Systems at Northeastern University. He is an active, frequent mentor of current PhD Project doctoral students, and he devotes significant time to youth ministry work in his hometown near Boston.

The pregnant college student who turned to Dr. Bradley for support is today a successful professional who occasionally stops by on campus to thank him. "Not because I told her what to do," says Dr. Bradley as he reflects on the importance of role models to minority undergraduates. "Just because I allowed her the opportunity to feel free to express her thoughts."

Road Less Traveled

Dr. Charles W. Richardson
Assistant Professor, Marketing
Clark Atlanta University

The littlest people in Dr. Charles W. Richardson's Marketing Principles class at the business school of Clark Atlanta University sit on the floor in the back, quietly sipping from juice boxes and playing with sticker books. Occasionally, they bicker over who gets to hold the Barbie doll.

They are the toddler sons and daughters of the students in Dr. Richardson's class, many of whom attend school at night while holding daytime jobs, several of them single parents with no one at home to care for the children.

Dr. Richardson, who could have accepted a professor's position in many other college settings, is most comfortable in this one. For decades, even before becoming a professor, he was deeply engaged in working with and at the nation's historically black colleges and universities (HBCUs). When he decided to leave a successful corporate career to become a business professor, there was no doubt that it would be at an HBCU.

Professor Richardson also teaches many students of traditional age at Clark Atlanta, and then the generational roles switch. With these students, it is their parents he gets to meet. This typically happens each spring at graduation, when many of his students introduce their parents to him after the ceremony with words that are almost identical:

"Mom, Dad, this is the professor I've been telling you about."

"I am," declares Dr. Richardson, "the road less traveled."

Dr. Richardson, who attended the first PhD Project conference in 1994, devotes several hours weekly to meet individually with students—even those who aren't enrolled in his class—who need support and guidance with academics and the transition to a career. He meets informally with 50 students a week and becomes so involved with their lives that he gets to know many of their parents. Challenges to succeed academically, family problems, help in planning a career: the professor takes on all these issues in addition to his teaching and research.

This is exactly what Dr. Richardson envisioned when he left business to pursue a PhD in marketing. As a corporate executive working long hours, he heard the calling to influence the next generation. When an opportunity to teach arose—first at an ethnically diverse community college serving nontraditional students in a New York City outer borough, then in similar settings in New Jersey—he grabbed it. Leaving his day job feeling exhausted and drained, he would emerge invigorated and energized from the algebra class he taught from 6:00 to 10:00 P.M. *"Mental note to self,"* he thought: *"This is what you will do next."*

In corporate life, he also participated actively in a nationwide program to provide business students at historically black colleges with successful role models. In that program, which was supported by his employer AT&T, he visited at least one historically black college a semester for 17 years. Eventually, AT&T loaned him out to the program, and he ran it full time.

By now he had visited more than 75 of the 100 or so HBCU campuses in the U.S. Consistently, he was inspired by the opportunities awaiting the students at these colleges if they could overcome the daunting challenges they faced.

Upon deciding that his next career turn would be to become a professor, he knew it would be at a historically black institution. It is not the dominant career path choice for most new professors, even those of African-American background, for a wide variety of personal and professional reasons. But it is where Charles Richardson expected to encounter the students whose lives he wanted to impact.

Three quarters of the students he encounters are first generation college attendees. They come with stories: "I'm finding more and more that students on the surface seem to be healthy, productive individuals—and the back story is anything but," he says.

"Every day I've got students, sitting in the front row smiling and engaged—great students. Unless you get to know them a little bit, you'll never hear the back story. When you do, there is more to it than meets the eye. The specifics vary, but they are facing significant challenges from various aspects of their personal lives—family circumstances, financial hardship, learning disabilities and more. I can see someone sleeping in class, and I know it's not because he was hanging out at the clubs—it's because he had to sleep in his car last night. These kinds of backgrounds challenge them in their quest to matriculate. I feel an obligation to be of service to them by sharing my insights and perspectives."

From where does this sense of obligation spring? "I was not exactly a 4.0 student myself," Dr. Richardson explains. "Actually, I was a bit of a knucklehead. So now, at HBCUs, where most of the faculty are not African-American, I can stand up and say, 'I haven't always been who I am today.' They can see what their teacher has done, and it creates a greater sense of belief that they can do it, too."

On the day he was interviewed for this profile, Dr. Richardson was preoccupied by the tangled tale of an undergraduate, her disabled mother, an unscrupulous housemate and an unsympathetic landlord. It was the messy drama of real life, far from the purview of a professor's job description. But the situation was disrupting the student's studies, so Dr. Richardson stepped forward to listen and offer help.

"I'm not doing this for the money," says Dr. Richardson. "I'm doing it to pass it along to the next generation. I'm going to do research. I'm going to get published. But I don't want my career to be judged solely on the basis of how many journals I'm in."

Dr. Richardson was one of three PhD Project professors named to prestigious American Council on Education (ACE) fellowships for 2014. The ACE Fellows program prepares promising faculty for senior leadership roles in academia.

Excerpts From Dr. Richardson's Personal Journal of Office Hours: One Typical Day, May 2013:

*Undergraduate junior: Needs job (related issues include possible eviction)—general encouragement, with more long-term support and guidance.

*Undergraduate senior: Failed Finance—advice on summer school and general encouragement on situation and future prospects.

*MBA student: On probation, 2nd semester grades sufficient to restore good standing, but disappointed in individual grade; also making change in major—general encouragement with career advice for new major area.

*Undergraduate senior: Going into Peace Corps—general advice on life/career post-Peace Corps service.

*Undergraduate junior: Failed Statistics—advice on summer school and senior year course selection with tutoring commitment for Statistics in fall.

*Undergraduate junior: General advising on course selection and Study Abroad participation.

*MBA student on probation: Better performance 2nd semester but insufficient to attain good standing—advice on appeal process and other options.

*MBA student: Course advising for summer school.

Dr. Richardson notes that he is consistently impressed by the "tenacity and ability to overcome" his mentees consistently display. "What I provide," he says, "is a platform to recognize those traits and minimize the impact of their challenges."

For Everyone Who Comes After You

Dr. Michael Clement
Accounting Doctoral Program Director, KPMG Faculty Fellow in Accounting Education, Professor of Accounting, University of Texas at Austin

"*I need to find a different way to achieve my goal,*" veteran University of Texas accounting professor Dr. Michael Clement thought as he surveyed the classroom of his Accounting 380K course, Financial Statement Analysis. There was not another African-American in the room.

One of the reasons Dr. Clement had leapt off a lucrative career path in investment banking years earlier was for the psychic reward of mentoring the next generation of minority students aiming for careers in business. But this particular semester, he realized, he was the only African-American in any of the three sections he taught.

Reflecting further, he knew that the problem wasn't unique to Texas. He had himself earned three degrees in business, one on each coast and one in the heartland. In all that time, it wasn't until his final year of PhD coursework that he encountered an African-American professor with a doctorate in accounting.

"There must be a way to reach these students," Dr. Clement thought. He contemplated a moment longer, then quickly dashed off an e-mail to the university's head basketball coach requesting a meeting.

At prominent Division I schools like the University of Texas at Austin, the basketball coach is among the reigning deities. Top athletics coaches at these colleges tend to take their meetings with university presidents, wealthy donors and the parents of highly prized high school prospects. As an 176accounting professor, Dr. Clement didn't expect much of a re1sponse to his e-mail. But in less than 10 minutes, an invitation to stop by and chat popped up in his in-box.

Ubiquitous on the UT Austin campus are reminders of what the university calls its core purpose: "To transform lives for the benefit of society." The potential for such transformations was high among student athletes, Dr. Clement reasoned: the Athletics Department was one place on campus not lacking in student diversity. Many student athletes, he also knew, were first-generation students. He had heard stories of first-generation student athletes inspiring siblings, cousins and even their own children: they were living proof of a college education's transformative value.

Dr. Clement's proposition to the coach was simple: he offered to strike up informal mentoring relationships with the team's African-American players, regardless of their major, to help them through academic issues they might face. The coach welcomed the idea, introduced the accounting professor to his team, and "things just took off from there," Dr. Clement recalls.

The role grew and stretched beyond basketball. Dr. Clement was named to serve as the university's Faculty Athletics Representative to the NCAA, a high-visibility position that makes him a pivotal bridge at Austin between collegiate athletics and academics. It places him at the heart of the ongoing societal debate over the balance between the two. It also places him at the side of the more than 500 Texas student athletes.

This positions him close to their ears, and this is what he tells them: "You are not here just for you. You are here for your families and everyone who comes after you—your children and your grandchildren."

He recounts how his grandmother persistently pushed his father—who would become a college professor—to pursue higher education, and how his father then inspired him to enter academia. "One day," he tells student athletes, "your grandson could be sitting here, and he won't know why he is here. But it will be because you made the decision to complete your degree here."

The students couldn't ignore Dr. Clement's presence and influence even if they wanted to. As Faculty Athletics Representative, he intervenes if their grades falter. He also signs off when classes have to be missed because of a road game.

Mostly, they listen appreciatively. Often, they approach him: something is going amiss in a class, or with the team, and they don't know what to do. As an African-American and a professor, he is the person they can count on for advice. After the issue at hand has been covered comes the reminder: "Stay in school and finish your degree."

The University of Texas produces world-class professional athletes; among the recent Longhorns to reach National Basketball Association superstardom were Kevin Durant and LaMarcus Aldridge. For these elite, a long line of advisers stands ready to assist and support them. Dr. Clement chooses to focus his attention on those students who are not superstars, for whom there is no such line of would-be advisers in waiting.

For the elite, the lure of leaving college prematurely to turn pro can be overwhelming. One athlete whom Dr. Clement befriended did rise to stardom, and he could not resist the siren call. He left Austin early to play in the NBA. However, Dr. Clement's frequent admonitions had resonated and hit home: before he left, he promised Dr. Clement he would return and complete his studies.

Regardless of his new status as professional basketball player, he doubled back to Austin and the classroom without fanfare, every summer. He completed his Bachelor's Degree as promised.

Himself a beneficiary of early career mentoring, much of it through PhD Project relationships, Dr. Clement actively mentors non-athlete undergraduates, as well as graduate students, of all backgrounds. "I believe there is a value to diversity," he says. "There is value in learning from different kinds of people.

"I think I can impact my white students, my Hispanic students, my Asian students and my Black students. Everybody benefits from being around different kinds of people."

Extending his influence across all three levels of academic study, he is also the director of the accounting department's highly ranked doctoral program. In that role, his formal responsibility is to participate in decisions about admissions, course selection, funding and scholarship. To that he adds a personal commitment to provide guidance and emotional support for the many doctoral candidates who need it.

At the September 1993 meeting that would lead to The PhD Project's creation, the then struggling doctoral student Michael Clement told his story to the assembled academics and business executives (see Origins), and the experience restored his flagging determination and confidence.

At that meeting he first articulated the thought that propelled him ahead, which he calls his "80 year test": "When I get to be 80 and look back at my life, how will I feel about what I've accomplished?"

Through the relationships Dr. Clement has formed via The PhD Project and in countless others, it is a thought he has passed on to new generations of doctoral students who were similarly inspired and who are today's and tomorrow's leaders in business education.

Three Women at a Table

Dr. Tiffany Barnett White
Associate Professor and Director of Graduate Study, Marketing
University of Illinois

The Gothic towers and rarefied intellectual atmosphere of Northwestern University in suburban Chicago envelop many a first-time visitor in a certain kind of imposing atmosphere. "Intimidating" is how some have described it.

For a visiting young woman raised in one of the rougher precincts of that town, possession of an MBA from another top university and sparkling success in the corporate world were not enough to spare her from thinking, "This place is much bigger than me or anything that I can imagine."

It was a frigid day in early January 1994, still 11 months before The PhD Project formally came into existence. Tiffany Barnett, going it alone, was exploring her prospects for becoming a marketing professor. Stepping from her car into the brisk lakeside air after the 40-minute drive from her Oak Park home, she thought, "This feels regal."

Ms. Barnett, already hooked on the appeal of joining the academy, had begun applying to doctoral programs when a Northwestern administrator had invited her to come out for a day of informational meetings. Readily accepting the offer, she wasn't sure what to expect—but one thing she certainly did not expect was to be introduced, late in the day, to not one or two, but *three* female African-American scholars in the marketing program.

"There were so few African-American women in the field," she recalls 20 years later. "And to walk into Northwestern, the heavy hitter and undisputed champ, and see three African-American women sitting around a table talking to *me*… It was the most amazing thing that had ever happened to me."

Some 750 miles from where The PhD Project was taking shape, the scene playing out at Northwestern would have cheered the founders had they known of it, because it corroborated one of their core beliefs: that more minorities would become business professors if they could see more people in those roles who looked like them.

The three women at the table were doctoral students Sonya Grier, Geraldine Henderson and Jacquelyn Thomas, who would all go on to become professors. They invited Ms. Barnett to discuss the conceptual underpinnings of her MBA thesis, and they listened intently in silent judgment of her potential as an academic. In the moment, the visitor feared she might be stumbling through her ideas somewhat awkwardly.

But when she finished, Ms. Henderson said, "Yes, you have what it takes. You're going to do just fine." Until that

moment, Ms. Barnett hadn't known that. It was a transformative moment for her.

"They were letting me into a conversation of really, really smart topics, and that made me feel confident that I could do this. I could join this club of very smart women who were going to achieve something and have success in this field."

"PhD—it's just three little letters," says the erstwhile intimidated applicant who is now Associate Professor of Marketing Dr. Tiffany Barnett White. "But it's a big word when you don't know anyone who has one. There was no PhD Project back then. I was going on a leap of faith."

That January seemed to be where her encounter with the three doctoral students would end. Accepted by the PhD program at Duke University, she headed there that fall, noting its business school's emerging strength in attracting African-American doctoral students.

But like so many fields, the world of marketing academe is a small and interconnected one. One day during her first year at Duke, Tiffany White dropped in to a presentation by a new PhD on the job market who was vying against established academics for a vacant marketing professorship. It was Geraldine Henderson.

Dr. Henderson's chances, statistically, were long. "She was competing with some of the world's best scholars," Dr. White recalls. Dr. Henderson won and accepted the position. For the remainder of her doctoral studies, Tiffany White had a role model and mentor who would become a lifelong colleague.

And when her turn came, and she was a marketing professor at the University of Illinois, Dr. White became a mentor in her own right. She quickly became an active, hands-on adviser to PhD Project marketing doctoral candidates. (At press time, one of those mentees had joined her department's PhD program at the University of Illinois and a second had just been admitted.) In addition, she would soon develop a deep interest—which evolved into a program—for introducing undergraduates to academic research.

The marketing experiment participants file silently into an austere cinderblock basement lab on the University of Illinois campus, taking seats along a row of computer screens. Directed by a pair of research assistants, the participants work through an exercise, which has them make simulated decisions about buying donuts. As they proceed, the research assistants observe closely, taking notes and guiding the participants through the session.

The research assistants are themselves undergraduates— no older than the test participants before them—and they are running the show. In fact, they have played a significant role in creating and designing the show.

What's missing from this seemingly routine picture? Professors, graduate research assistants, senior researchers—in other words, all the expected "adult" administration of an academic experiment.

This unusual effort in undergraduate empowerment was the brainchild of Dr. White, who became a pioneer in meaningfully involving undergraduate marketing students in serious, publishable academic research.

In the donut experiment, undergraduates Emily Retzer and Rachel Johnston have designed many of the key experiment components long before the day they administer the session to participants.

Beginning in a research brainstorming session—often held in Dr. White's home—they have designed the experiment, developed controls, designed and organized the visuals and computer displays and choreographed the session. If they decide the test product for a project is donuts, they'll invent the wacky flavor names. If it's shampoo, they'll design the product label and packaging. When the data comes in, they will help analyze and interpret it.

The students know they'd better craft their designs with great care and precision: their work must stand up to the rigorous scrutiny of the peer-reviewed journals for which the experiments are bound.

"I am learning so much about the role marketing research plays in marketing professionally," later enthuses Ms. Johnston, a marketing major. "The hands-on experience expands what I learn in the classroom."

What Dr. White's students think they are getting from this program is verified by their former peers who have completed it. "I'm sure it helped me get my job," says 2007 graduate Roxanne Chow, who became an auditor with a Big 4 firm. "Even though I didn't go into marketing, it got me from a technical level to an analytic level, looking at things from the overall perspective. That's what I have to do in my job, and I could talk about it in my interviews."

Dr. White's research mentorship flows from a deeply engrained spirit of giving back. On her official College of Business biography, Dr. White describes herself, along with her academic credentials, credits and official titles, as a "marketing mentor." It is an apt description of the role she has created for herself.

"I just surrounded myself with people who believed in me," Dr. White once told a campus publication. "Now I try to be somebody who encourages my students and says, 'You can do it.'"

Impacting the Community

Anything in the World

Dr. dt ogilvie
Distinguished Professor of Urban Entrepreneurship
Rochester Institute of Technology

Dr. Ian Williamson
Associate Dean and Director, Asia Pacific Social Impact
Leadership Center
Melbourne Business School

The year was 1993, and the seeds that would become The PhD Project were just taking form as a new PhD went on the job market and interviewed for a management professor position.

At many of the campuses she visited, Dr. dt ogilvie looked in vain for faculty members of color in the business school. Rarely did she see one. "The numbers were very sparse," she recalls of those early years. "I remember going to the Academy of Management meetings—you'd look over the room and you might see a person of color or two, but it was rare. We all knew each other and we gravitated to each other."

Dr. ogilvie found employment at Rutgers University and inevitably, she and The PhD Project found each other. At the second conference in 1995, Dr. ogilvie was a featured panelist. Sitting in the audience was someone she had met four years earlier: Ian Williamson, a retailing manager who had been considering a career switch to academia for some time. When someone asked Dr. ogilvie if the rigors and challenges of earning a business doctorate were "worth it," she replied, "It's more than worth it. Once you get a PhD you can do anything in the world with it." Ian Williamson took special note of her answer.

The words and the idea resonated with Williamson, who locked them into his memory and mindset. In the ensuing years as he pursued his doctorate, entered the professoriate and received promotions, Dr. ogilvie would become his go-to mentor for letters of recommendation, advice and overall guidance.

And when an unusual opportunity came along—a teaching, research and administrative position at the Melbourne Business School in Australia—the words Dr. Williamson had heard many years earlier reverberated as a challenge: "Anything in the world."

"If that is true," he reasoned, "and I don't actually try to do 'anything in the world,' then I am underutilizing this degree."

Dr. Williamson pursued and won the position. He says, "It has opened the floodgates of opportunity for me."

Dr. ogilvie has mentored so many doctoral students and junior faculty since that 1995 conference, that she was named to The PhD Project Hall of Fame in 2013. The mentorship she offered Dr. Williamson would be indistinguishable from the countless others she took on, except for the fact that mentor and mentee's paths eventually converged and gave rise to a remarkable and fruitful synergy. Their joint scholarship is lifting the prospects of two widely disparate underserved communities.

Building a career at Rutgers, Dr. ogilvie came to feel she had found a home. Over the years, academia's seeming allergy to minority business professors, which she had found so distressing in her job search, was starting to ease thanks to The PhD Project's work. Here was where ability and determination met opportunity and need. Rutgers Business School was not only located right in the heart of downtown Newark, New Jersey, but through her efforts, it was actively engaged in economic development partnerships with the community. Dr. ogilvie founded The Center for Urban Entrepreneurship & Economic Development (CUEED). Its goal: to create a world class research hub that would engage and partner with the surrounding community to create, encourage and support economic growth.

To do that research, Dr. ogilvie attracted top academic talent from leading universities to the center. As a result, Rutgers Business School was acquiring a reputation for an increasingly diverse faculty—thanks in no small part to her persuasive recruiting efforts of PhD Project professors. And, as icing on the cake, Rutgers Business School seemed to welcome faculty with social and community interests, and to encourage academic research into minority-related topics.

Newark, with all its socioeconomic ills and challenges, "was our laboratory," she recalls. Rebuilding it—through the growth of entrepreneurship—was the aim. First generation entrepreneurs came to the center to be taught sound approaches to successful entrepreneurship by Rutgers faculty and other subject matter experts. They left it with actionable business and growth plans.

The year Dr. ogilvie launched the center—2008—was not a fortuitous one. But when the long recession that began that year finally eased, most of the businesses in her center had endured. Also thriving were the undergraduates coming through the school's new minor in entrepreneurship, as well as a two-block patch of downtown targeted for rebirth by Dr. ogilvie's institute. The center had swiftly emerged as an influential nexus for research and community-oriented business education outreach.

Watching all this carefully was Dr. Williamson. Despite numerous entreaties by Dr. ogilvie to join the exciting work in Newark, his sights were set farther away. "Anything in the world" had evolved for him into increasing appreciation for the opportunities and challenges of global business. This awareness came to him in part from the large representation in his classes of international students from all over the world. Their discussions in and out of class often revolved around experiences and perspectives that were, literally and figuratively, foreign to him. They were the conversations and contributions of young adults who had left their home countries to explore business issues in a different culture and setting.

"If I am to remain relevant as an academic and contribute to this conversation," he thought, "I need to experience what they are experiencing. If they can do it, I should be able to do it also." These realizations prompted Dr. Williamson to accept the position at the Melbourne Business School in Australia, which was just then creating a center to examine new ways for a business school to address social challenges. In 2009, he became its first director.

Melbourne Business School's leaders were prescient and enlightened enough to conceive the Asia Pacific Social Impact Leadership Center, but they were not knowledgeable enough to build it by themselves. They gave Dr. Williamson carte blanche to invent the program. His response gratified them profoundly: "I'm coming with a template."

But first, he headed to Newark.

Dr. Williamson identified that one critical issue for his center to address was the severe economic disadvantage in the indigenous Australian community. The physical environment and demographic characteristics of the Aboriginal population differed from the urban setting of Newark, but the issues were very similar: like the minority urbanites in Newark, the indigenous groups of Australia had strong entrepreneurial traits but little formal education or experience in business. Dr. Williamson spent two months in Newark with Dr ogilvie, observing what she had built and learning the lessons of what she had accomplished: "I had seen what worked, and it was a matter of contextualizing it with the Australian experience."

At Melbourne, he established an initiative called Murra—the Aboriginal word for fishnet, as in the gathering of native entrepreneurs by the business school in order to educate them. Its curriculum and underlying principles dovetailed closely with those of the Newark center.

Today, the Newark center and its counterpart in Melbourne create synergies that transcend borders. The two centers collaborate on research and problem-solving. Dr. ogilvie has introduced innovative approaches that were new to Australia, both to the university and local government leaders. Many of her ideas are being implemented.

The collaboration is a two-way street. The Melbourne center has become an incubator for social entrepreneurship, the notion of community and non-governmental organizations applying business methodologies to grow and thrive. Rutgers management professor Dr. Jeffrey Robinson, a PhD Project professor from New York University whom Dr. ogilvie recruited to Rutgers as assistant director of CUEED, visited

Melbourne to teach Dr. Williamson's students and interact with faculty. He returned home with new ideas that helped fuel his development of another new CUEED initiative, the New Jersey Social Innovation Institute. Economic and social organizations on two continents are being enhanced and strengthened by the intellectual cross-fertilization that continues to unfold in Newark and Melbourne.

As a professor, CUEED director and former associate provost at Rutgers, Dr. ogilvie was having a tangible impact. But new opportunities do come along, and in 2012 Dr. ogilvie went to Rochester Institute of Technology (RIT), where she served for two years as dean of the business school. During her deanship, the school's academic rankings improved and undergraduate applications increased. But among her first acts in that role: establishing a Center for Urban Entrepreneurship in downtown Rochester, modeled after Newark, to contribute to the resurgence of that city. The center, scheduled to open in 2015 but already offering programs at interim locations, will enlarge RIT's presence in downtown Rochester. Its goal is to help businesses with growth potential connect with area investors and sources of capital. Dr. ogilvie was named in 2014 to chair its advisory committee and serve as Distinguished Professor of Urban Entrepreneurship.

In April 2014, Dr. Robinson was named the new Academic Director & Senior Fellow at The Center for Urban Entrepreneurship & Economic Development at Rutgers Business School, following in Dr. ogilvie's footsteps.

Dr. ogilvie continues mentoring doctoral students and junior faculty associated with The PhD Project. Among those she helped navigate the long path from PhD student to employment as a professor was a young Hispanic scholar from Southern California who shared her passion for reaching beyond campus borders to an underserved community....

Saturday Mornings

Dr. Angélica Gutiérrez
Assistant Professor of Management
Loyola Marymount University

Angélica Gutiérrez learned from experience, at age eight, how stereotyping and prejudice can deprive ethnic minorities of educational opportunity. Her mother was summoned to the elementary school principal's office one day to hear that her daughter had a learning disability and would be transferred to a special education program.

Fortunately for Angélica, her mother instantly recognized this assessment for the nonsense it was. She calmly explained to the principal that, no, the issue was that English was not her daughter's native language. Angélica remained in the school and went on to excel there and in all the schools that would follow.

But it wasn't until late in high school that she fully appreciated that she could accomplish great things. Running for student body president, she concluded her campaign speech with an unusual request. She told the students she would one day run for President of the United States, and she asked them to remember to vote for her then too. Her bold request was not met with the laughs she expected; rather, the crowd responded with cheers and applause.

Angélica went on to undergraduate study at UCLA and then earned a Master's in Public Policy at the University of Michigan. Not long after, she switched career plans and disciplines to pursue a doctorate in management, back at UCLA.

The idea of becoming a professor wasn't completely new; it dated back to an undergraduate experience. As a student peer counselor, one to whom freshmen and sophomores (especially minorities planning to study business) flocked for advice, Dr. Gutiérrez recalls the troubling pattern she discerned:

"They would find me early on, their first or second quarter, and they were always very enthusiastic. They were eager to get into the business major and start taking courses, because they all had incredible dreams about someday launching their own business or becoming an executive at a high profile corporation."

"But I noticed that in their second year, many of them decided to change majors. It was disheartening to see them lose their motivation, and I would ask them why. It turned out they no longer felt they had what it took to complete the coursework. They had great difficulties with their economics classes.

"I would encourage them to visit their professors, to ask how they might better prepare for the next exam, or provide a better paper next time."

The response she frequently heard disturbed her. But it was the spark that led to her discovery of her calling: "They said they did not feel comfortable, as ethnic minorities, going to see their professors. They would say, 'I feel intimidated. My professor is from a different group, and I don't see how I can engage them in a conversation.'"

After hearing variations on the same doleful story from several students, she grew frustrated, thinking: "If I were that professor, I would not only provide them with extra instruction; I would do everything possible to mentor them and encourage them to continue as a business major.

"And then at one point I just said to myself: *Angélica, why don't you become that business professor you wish they had?*"

The Saturday Business Academy, an offshoot of a UCLA community outreach program, targets college-potential high school students from at-risk communities in south Los Angeles. As early as 8:00 A.M. on Saturdays, they meet with teachers and young professionals for a full morning of college preparation and coaching. Even as a doctoral student facing a daunting work and study load, Dr. Gutiérrez would conduct workshops on negotiations at the Saturday morning academy.

"These students will be interviewing for jobs; they will be negotiating," she says. "They will have to negotiate effectively, whether it is for an employment offer, the purchase of a car, over a contract, or for an apartment. These are skills they can learn, and I present them."

Many in the group have heard little, during their youth, about the various professions and jobs that exist in the business sector. Dr. Gutiérrez walks them through an overview of the many opportunities that could await them in business. But first, she cautions, they need to acquire their diplomas and degrees.

In this program and in regular visits back to her own LA-area alma mater, Dr. Gutiérrez plants seeds of encouragement for the teenagers to attend college and earn that diploma. Wherever she detects interest or aptitude, she encourages them to consider studying business. One year, a high school junior responded not only to the message, but more specifically, wanted to matriculate at UCLA. Dr. Gutiérrez coached and supported her on every step of the admissions process, and through the subsequent four years of earning a bachelor's degree in economics. The young woman became a successful professional and, at press time, was planning to apply to an M.B.A. program.

"She is going to excel in her M.B.A. program just as she excelled as an undergraduate," Dr. Gutiérrez predicts confidently.

Since becoming a professor, in addition to her teaching and mentoring, Dr. Gutiérrez conducts innovative research and serves government. She explores issues of diversity and inclusion relating to various aspects of business management, notably recruitment and hiring. In 2013, she began working with the City of Los Angeles on examining its recruitment, selection and retention of women minority workers.

Dr. Gutiérrez was one of 10 Hispanic women recognized as the "Next Generation Latina" by Latina Magazine, *an award that honors Latinas who have made a significant impact as role models, mentors and leaders. She was one of*

20 Hispanic women named a "Latina of Influence" by Hispanic Lifestyle *magazine.*

Robots and Bingo

Dr. Laura Hall
Associate Professor, Information Systems
University of Texas at El Paso

For 15 years, Dr. Laura Hall, an Hispanic-American charter participant in the PhD Project, has exemplified paying it forward by taking her Information Systems students back—back to elementary school settings like those they once experienced.

There, Dr. Hall's University of Texas at El Paso (UTEP) students use fun and games to introduce children as young as pre-K to computer literacy and robotics. More than 350 such community-based projects have taken place under her tutelage, and they are a win-win: as the elementary schoolers learn, so do the college students who interact with them.

The University of Texas Regents' Outstanding Teaching Award was bestowed on Dr. Hall in 2013 for this innovative work. The honor, which carries a monetary award of $25,000, is among the nation's largest and most competitive award for outstanding faculty performance.

According to Dr. Hall, El Paso is a school system with many technological shortcomings: "They don't have people with the expertise to fix computer systems. These are excellent projects for my students, because they can go in and do all that for free.

"My students are so talented that I'm saying, 'Why am I the sage on the stage? Why are they just listening to me? Why am I not taking advantage of the skills that these students have?'"

In El Paso public schools, Dr. Hall's undergraduates play a "Technology Bingo" game to teach Head Start children about computing. They build robots with elementary school children, and they build Internet safety awareness among middle school students.

"The objective is for teams to build a robot and design a presentation for children," says Dr. Hall, a tenured Associate Professor. "The goal is of course to interest them in robots, but the hidden agenda is to plant the seed that college can be fun and that they need to go."

The program, she notes, also prepares her undergraduates "to be strong role models for other underrepresented minority students in the region." When they go into high schools, it is to deliver a direct sales pitch for attending college—and majoring in business.

In El Paso, Dr. Hall notes, "25% of the population has less than a ninth grade education. Only 11% graduate from college with a Bachelor's degree. I can change this. I change it through my attention and support of these students."

Over 15 years, Dr. Hall and her students have brought their program to virtually every elementary school in El Paso, and for a 30-mile radius around it.

UTEP is an Hispanic-serving institution with many first-generation and non-traditional students. In addition to her teaching and research, Dr. Hall is faculty adviser to some nationally honored student organizations that focus on professional development.

"No student will leave my classroom without knowing how to begin the pathway to a higher level of education and promise," she says.

This commitment extends all the way to doctoral studies: Dr. Hall has encouraged many of her students to follow her footsteps and consider becoming a business professor.

"At UTEP, I have been able to reach thousands of underrepresented students with the message that there is no reason that YOU can't be a business school professor or anything else that you want to be," she says.

Dr. Hall, who has been on the faculty at UTEP since 1996, traces her desire to teach back to third grade, when the teacher thrilled her by reading to the class the Helen Keller story. Early in her career, she became a special education teacher. Then came a stint in business, after which she recognized that she would prefer teaching college. By this time, though, Dr. Hall was a single mother of three preschool aged children. She sought advice from a favorite professor in her MBA program. "You shouldn't even try," the professor told her.

The professor imagined that Hall's family situation would be too formidable a barrier to overcome. Moreover, he cautioned, the academic rigor of earning a doctorate would simply be too difficult for her.

Dr. Hall rejected his counsel and in short order applied—to Harvard and Stanford.

She did not get in to either, but Florida State University admitted her the following year. The children were aged one, four and five. Divorce was pending. Debt was following her.

With her family hundreds of miles away, she proceeded on her own to earn her PhD and raise three children. Partway through her journey, The PhD Project was formed, and she attended its first meeting (see Origins).

There, she says, she heard "things I had never heard before: how important I was, how much difference I could make, how I could help others follow their dreams—and all I had to do was keep on my track, share what I knew with others and reach a hand backwards."

As a doctoral student and then a professor, Dr. Hall did just that. No PhD Project doctoral student in her discipline enters a program, passes comprehensive exams, defends a dissertation or graduates without receiving a congratulatory email from her. She attends virtually every meeting of The PhD Project and the Information Systems Doctoral Students Association, and she rarely fails to tell the story of her personal journey. The crowd invariably falls silent when she reaches the part about the three young children and the debt. Afterwards, someone usually tells her, "I will never feel sorry for myself again."

Dr. Hall has become her discipline's "go-to" mentor for single mothers in The PhD Project. "I must have gotten a hundred people through," she jokes, "because they decide that if I could do it, they could do it."

Unlocking

Dr. Adriane Randolph
Associate Professor, Information Systems
Kennesaw State University

The most severely impacted patients with spinal cord injury or brain disease are said to be "locked in." Completely paralyzed, they can neither speak nor move, not even to shake their head.

PhD Project Professor Dr. Adriane Randolph uses her technology expertise to unlock them.

Through trailblazing research into brain-computer interfacing, she develops systems that enable these patients to communicate with their loved ones and caregivers.

This might never have happened had it not been for the peer support and encouragement she received through The PhD Project.

Adriane Randolph was a successful global business consultant when she realized she needed to be having a greater impact "on the lives of real people." When the infant field of brain-computer interfacing attracted her attention, it was still largely the stuff of science fiction. But, she discovered, serious academic research was promising to turn sci-fi into reality.

She enrolled in a doctoral program in information systems and dove deeply into the new field. But while she clearly envisioned the unfolding of a new sub-discipline in information systems academic research, others did not yet grasp it. "How is this information systems?" other scholars would ask her.

And so the realities of the academic world collided with her passion: how would she get published in major journals, or even gain academic recognition, from research on a topic not yet accepted as a legitimate niche?

She wondered if she might be making a mistake.

So, she asked her colleagues in the PhD Project's Information Systems Doctoral Students Association for guidance.

There, she found strong support and encouragement to follow her dream and her path.

"This is really interesting work," they told her. "Stick with it—you are impacting lives. You are really helping people."

And so she did.

Today, with brain-computer interfacing an accepted research topic and Dr. Randolph respected as a leader in it, she is grateful that she did. And she is appreciative of The PhD Project's contribution to her decision.

"I don't think I would have had the in-field success I now have without The PhD Project," she says. "I am able to publish in mainstream information systems outlets. That has been through the championing of people I have met through The PhD Project."

Dr. Randolph, as Director of the BrainLab at Kennesaw State University, and her students bring their pioneering, nationally recognized work right into the homes of patients.

The work is based on the same technology that marketing researchers use to learn what consumers *really* think: it captures and reads brainwaves. Utilizing it, Dr. Randolph can train a parent, in the family home, to place an electrode cap on an injured child's head. The cap, connected to a device called a bio-amplifier, turns up the brain waves' "volume" and transmits them to a computer as the patient uses thought to spell out the words she wishes to communicate. The computer translates the waves into words the parent can read on a screen.

Sometimes, the parent reads a message like "Please turn the TV off," or "Please look at the sore on my leg." Sometimes the words are, "I love you, Mom." These are the moments when Dr. Randolph takes special pleasure in appreciating the decision she made, a decade earlier, to stick with her passion.

"I once realized that I am bringing hope to families that might have lost it before I arrived," she says. "When you're doing experiments in the lab, you can under-appreciate that part. But when you're in the field working with families, you can see it."

The work that Dr. Randolph and others are doing is on its way to becoming mainstream, with commercial applications starting to emerge. Before long, caregivers won't need a team of researchers at their side to direct their interactions with patients: they will be able to place a headset on the patient and operate a user-friendly system.

"It's exciting to be part of the initial ground level of brain-computer interfacing, but it is also humbling," Dr. Randolph says. "It is humbling to think of bringing hope to families, and laying the groundwork for widespread use of this in the future.

"I love that I am helping people and impacting lives—that I am helping patients communicate with their loved ones to say, 'I love you'."

Behind, Beside and Ahead: A Model for Mentoring and Networking

By Dr. Dawn H. Pearcy
Professor, Marketing, Eastern Michigan University

Behind us: Mentoring

As faculty members, we can help guide current (and prospective) doctoral students, help them avoid some of the pitfalls of doctoral studies, serve as role models and provide encouragement. The latter is especially important. Sometimes just hearing an encouraging word from someone, who has experienced the challenges of doctoral studies and succeeded, is helpful in renewing one's confidence and determination to apply to a PhD program and/or successfully complete it.

Faculty members can actively seek out opportunities to collaborate with doctoral students on research projects and publications. Faculty members can work with doctoral students to help them develop and cultivate their research skills and navigate the publication process. This network is especially important if the opportunities for faculty-student collaboration and guidance are lacking at the student's own institution.

Beside us: Network/collaborate with others

Current doctoral students should develop networks with other students—within one's discipline—to provide support, share ideas, capitalize on each other's strengths, give/receive guidance and build a rapport for future research collaboration. Current doctoral students will be future colleagues.

Across disciplines and across institutions, it is also possible to gain different perspectives about one's own research and set the foundation for cross-disciplinary research when this type of networking takes place.

The PhD Project does a great job in providing a professional network, as well as the opportunity to develop strong social bonds. We should never underestimate the value of social relationships, as they help support and sustain us during the doctoral program, contribute to our professional life afterwards and often result in the development of lifelong friendships.

Ahead of us

Current doctoral students should develop their networks and look for several types of mentors.
• Faculty members who actively participate in The PhD Project serve as role models, as well as sources of guidance about navigating the program, research and publishing and balancing doctoral studies with family life, etc.
• Faculty members at one's institution. Early on, doctoral students should develop relationships with professors within

their department. This is important in identifying faculty members with similar research interests who might ultimately become dissertation committee members (or the chair). In addition, networking with faculty members outside of one's department provides access to mentors with varied areas of expertise, skills and resources.

• Doctoral students who are further ahead of you in the program. Other doctoral students can help with advice on preparation for the major milestones that lie ahead (e.g. comprehensive exams, preparing to enter the job market), as well as tips for success and approaches to avoiding the pitfalls of the program. They are a great resource because they have recent experience.

• Administrators. If one has aspirations of ultimately pursuing a career in administration, it is never too early to create a network with individuals in those positions.

Based on a presentation by Dr. Pearcy to The PhD Project Marketing Doctoral Students Association.

The Next Frontier: Moving AHEAD

Fewer than 20 dean positions at majority-serving university business schools at press time were held by African-Americans, Hispanic-Americans or Native Americans. Even at minority serving university business schools, fewer than 25 were deans at Historically Black Colleges and Universities (HBCUs) or Hispanic Serving Institutions (HSIs). In total about 3% of university business school deans' positions are held by African-Americans, Hispanic-Americans or Native Americans.

Looking at the current state of diversity in administrative positions, the next logical step for The PhD Project was to create diversity in these roles. That is why, in 2010, The Project launched a new initiative to increase diversity at the next level—business school administration.

Project AHEAD (Achieving Higher Education Administration Diversity) provides information, encouragement and support for African-American, Hispanic-American and Native American business school professors who wish to advance to the positions of department chair, associate dean, dean and other leadership roles. Many minority business professors are well qualified to be business school administrators, because they typically come to academia from successful corporate careers.

Project AHEAD holds informational programs, webinars for aspiring administrators, group and one-on-one mentoring, support and networking opportunities for PhD Project professors. In recent years, executive recruiters have begun participating. Minority and majority deans, department chairs and other administrators affiliated with The PhD Project provide services on a voluntary basis. Many of these activities take place at and around the summer Doctoral Students Association conferences and professional conferences that many PhD Project professors attend.

The PhD Project Deans' Advisory Board supports and participates in the initiative. Its members are Dr. Carolyn Callahan, former Dean, College of Business, University of Louisville; Dr. Quiester Craig, Dean (Emeritus) School of Business and Economics, North Carolina Agricultural and Technical State University; Dr. dt ogilvie, former Dean, Saunders College of Business, Rochester Institute of Technology; Dr. John A. Elliott, Dean, University of Connecticut School of Business; Dr. Eli Jones, Dean, Sam Walton College of Business, University of Arkansas; Dr. Andrew Policano, Director of the Center for Investment and Wealth Management, The Paul Merage School of Business, University of California Irvine; and Dr. Melvin Stith, Dean, Whitman School of Business, Syracuse University. They have all seen through The PhD Project how a minority professor can make a significant impact in the classroom. Dean Craig, speaking for the group, noted: "That influence increases dramatically as one moves up the ladder to administrative positions."

Mark Dawkins, Associate Dean of the Terry College of Business at the University of Georgia and a longtime PhD Project participant, predicts that "The AHEAD program is going to play a really important role in getting our graduates ready to assume roles of leadership at their institutions."

Given the demographic shifts taking place in the U.S. and in higher education, he says, "From my perspective, we need to have more people of color, not only in the front of the classroom, but also making decisions about the priorities of the university and the direction that each university takes.

"You can't make those decisions unless you're seated at the table," he adds. "That's why it was important for me to take an administrative role. It helps set the direction for your college and university. I think I've been able to do that in my five years as an associate dean."

Index

A

Abraham, Dorothea La "Chon," 126
Academy of Management (AOM), 162
Affirmative action, 18, 172–73
African-American Accounting Doctoral Students Association (AADSA), 39, 52–53, 56. *See also* The PhD Project Doctoral Students Associations
African-American Accounting Doctoral Students Scholarship (KPMG), 29–30
African-Americans
    CPAs as % of U.S. population, 28
    doctoral accounting students in 1994, 51
    faculty representation in 1990s, 9, 20
    faculty representation in 2014, 60
    representation in business school administration, 185–87
    student representation on campus, 78
    underrepresentation in the workplace, 18–19
Aldridge, LaMarcus, 153
Alino, Nelson, 112–13
Alvarez-Mourey, James ("Dr. Quatro"), 68
American Accounting Association (AAA), 27–28, 51–53
American Assembly of Collegiate Schools of Business, 1
American Council on Education Fellows (2013-14), 99–100
American Indian Higher Education Consortium, 107–08
American Institute of Certified Public Accounts, 27–29, 114–15
American Marketing Association (AMA), 82
Arizona State University, 113–14
Association to Advance Collegiate Schools of Business (AACSB), 1–2, 11–12, 25–26, 32, 43, 61, 68
AACSB International, 5, 7
Athletics, linking business education to, 141–42, 150–54
Australia, Melbourne Business School, 165–67

B

Benford, Tanya, 65
Black Enterprise (magazine), 55
Blackwell, James, 20
Bradley, Randy, 122–25, 138–44
Brain-computer interfacing, 178–81
Brown, Paul, 65

Fredericks, Elisa, 65
Fulbright Program
    Fulbright Scholars
        Dr. Dorothea La "Chon" Abraham, 126
        Dr. Efosa C. Idemudia, 126
        Dr. José Antonio Rosa, 126
        Dr. Renée Pratt, 122–26
    Fulbright Specialists
        Dr. Stephanie Yates, 126

G

Games, business education through, 174–76
Garcia, Luis A., 65
Garcia, Rosanna, 65
Gladstone, Joseph, 102–09
Globalization, response to, 2, 18, 25–26, 28–30, 47, 83, 128, 133, 165
Gonzaga University, 102
Gonzalez, Jorge, 65
Graduate Management Admission Council, 5, 25, 33, 43, 54, 61
Graduate Management Admission Test (GMAT), 25, 77
Grantham, Kimberly, 65
Grier, Sonya, 86, 156–57
Gutiérrez, Angélica, 169–73

H

Hall, Laura, 44, 57, 60, 62–65, 74, 174–77
Hammond, Theresa, 16–17, 19, 28, 72, 73
Henderson, Geraldine Rosa, 82–89, 156–57
Hispanic Lifestyle (magazine), 172–73
Hispanic Serving Institutions (HSI), 185
Hispanic-Americans
    addressing educational needs of children, 174–76
    eligibility for scholarship program, 29–30
    faculty representation in 1990s, 9, 20
    faculty representation in 2014, 60
    increasing U.S. population growth, 26
    recognition of role models and mentors, 172–73
    representation in business school administration, 185–87
    student representation on campus, 78
    underrepresentation in business disciplines, 42–43
    underrepresentation in the workplace, 18–19
Historically Black Colleges and Universities, 22–23, 130, 145–48, 185

Howard University, 84–85, 88–89

I

Idemudia, Efosa C., 126

J

Jackson, Joyce, 65
Johnson, Olenda, 62–64, 74
Johnson, Peter, 53, 73
Johnston, Rachel, 158–59
Jones, Eli, 186
Journal of Management Education, 106–07
Journal of Public Policy and Marketing (AMA), 82

K

Katerberg, Ralph, 46, 56, 67–68
Kennedy, Deanna M., 102–09
Kennesaw State University, 96–97, 178, 180
KPMG
    recruitment and hiring needs, 18–19, 25–26
    support of The PhD Project, 67, 200
KPMG Foundation
    accounting research grant program, 19, 31, 38
    adding early sponsors and support, 43–44
    creation of scholarship program, 28–30
    holding the St. Louis summit (1993), 32–33, 154
    Montvale AADSA meeting (August, 1994), 52–53
    Montvale meeting (January, 1994), 37–43
    role as a founding sponsor, 5–8

L

Labors From the Heart: Mission and Ministry in a Catholic University
    (Poorman, ed.), 94–95
Lacy, Jo Yvette, 65
Latina Magazine, 172–73
Lawrence, Karl, 65
Lawson, Stephanie, 134
Lewis, William, 65
Lopez, Thomas, 68, 73, 110–15
Loyola Marymount University, 74, 169
Lucas, Leyland, 65

M

Malloy, Alisha ("Dr. Double"), 67
Martinez, Patricia Garcia, 62, 64, 65, 74
Massiah, Carolyn, 116–19, 133
McCoy, Nicole, 135
McDougal, Karen, 65
Melbourne Business School (Australia), 162, 165–67
Mentoring. *See* Role models and mentoring
Merchant, Sylnovie, 65
Milano, Bernie
    about creation of The Phd Project, 5–6, 72
    advancing the vision of diversity, 1–4, 31–32, 71–72
    continuing the Project leadership, 74
    holding the first Montvale meeting (1994), 37–42
    holding the St. Louis summit (1993), 32–36
    induction into Hall of Fame, 67
    KPMG Foundation role, 18, 37
    KPMG recruiting role, 1, 71
    KPMG scholarship program, 28–30
    planning the 1994 conference, 46–48
    as role model, mentor, inspiration, 19, 72, 200
    securing academe support, 54–55, 61, 63
    securing sponsors and funding, 49–50
    sharing the credit, 198
Minority Doctoral Student Associations, 11–12
Minority MBA (magazine), 55
Minority Summer Institute (MSI), 21, 23–25, 32–33, 74
Montague, Norma, 135
Morgan State University, 93–94
Mosley, Alisa, 65, 67
Mumpower, Jeryl, 131

N

National Association of Black Accountants (NABA), 80–81
National Basketball Association (NBA), 153
National Black MBA Association, 54–55
National Collegiate Athletic Association (NCAA), 152
National Committee to Recruit African-Americans into Accounting
    Doctoral Programs, 37–43
National Science Foundation (NSF), 128–31
Native Americans
    eligibility for scholarship program, 29–30

Acknowledgments

If, as Bernie Milano suggests, The PhD Project has a million fingerprints, this book has a thousand.

Everyone profiled in these pages gave generously of their time, not only in sharing their stories but with invaluable insights and guidance for the retelling of them here. In many cases, now-successful professors recounted not-so-impressive episodes of early career near-defeat. They didn't have to do that, and each was reminded of this. Each insisted on doing so, and all cited the same reason: to show the next generation that obstacles can be overcome. I know from our experience following publication of the first PhD Project book, Living The Dream, that someone, somewhere, will read one of these stories and decide to become a business professor because of it. Someone else, at a moment of challenge in their doctoral studies, will read another of these stories and be inspired to continue.

The PhD Project, though brilliantly conceived, was nonetheless improvised on the fly in its early development. Little formal documentation of its formation was preserved. To recount the story some 20-plus years later, The PhD Project convened five conference calls in which most of the original players relived their memories. This made it possible to piece together more or less comprehensively, for the first time, the history – and the context of the early 1990s in which it unfolded. Thank you to each one: Matt Anderson, Neil Bosland, Carolyn Callahan, Nicole Chestang, Michael Clement, Quiester Craig, Mark Dawkins, Bob Elliot, John Fernandes, Theresa Hammond, Peter Johnson, Ralph Katerberg, Denny Reigle, Sandra Shelton, George Siedel, Melvin Stith and Peter Thorp.

I and my team have been privileged to work with The PhD Project for the entire twenty years. My partner in crime through it all, and the person to whom I turn whenever something is so audaciously daunting that it scares me, is Lisa King. This book was one such project, and I knew there would be no pulling it off unless she took charge. She did, and then some, to my deep gratitude. Thanks to Kayla Flynn for her diligence and care in providing editorial assistance at many levels. Longtime friend and colleague Dan Bosko volunteered his time to read every chapter, his wise observations enhanced this book in many ways. Thanks to Andrea Glass for her copyediting and Galen Schroeder for his indexing. Thanks to Achilles Perry, process architect par excellence.

The idea that led to the cover design hit me when a PhD Project meeting, called to review the program's mission and vision statement, had the unintended consequence of setting my mind roaming. Artist Bonnie Astor splendidly performed the critical task of capturing my mental pictures on paper, and graphic designer Kathie Rokita executed the final product superbly.

The PhD Project team drives it all, this book included. They are responsible for the amazing success of the Project.

Thank you to Tara Perino for overall excellence, and for assiduously tracking down all manner of long-forgotten documents, facts and details. Thanks to Marie Zara for her strong editorial sense and ability to spot a story line that veered from its truest path. Also to Joanne Berry, Zoila Jurado and Myrna Varner.

KPMG via KPMG Foundation covers all administrative overhead of running The PhD Project, in addition to its huge direct financial support. There would be no PhD Project without them. Everyone involved in the Project owes them their appreciation.

Bernie Milano, as Carolyn Callahan noted, "is one of those people who can identify what you can do, long before you think you can do it." I can vouch for this. Bernie's insights inform virtually every page of this book. Many passages and ideas appearing on these pages are the results of seeds Bernie planted during our planning process; something I often I didn't even realize until the words started flowing from my keyboard. Bernie has been more than a client for these two decades. He has been a role model, inspiration and mentor to me as well as to all who pass through The PhD Project. All readers, take note: When facing a challenging moment, the question to ask oneself is, "What would Bernie do?"

Ned Steele
New York, NY

"We've been successful to this point, but we've only touched the tip of the iceberg. There's so much more to be accomplished."
– *Dr. Randy Bradley*

To Learn More,
Visit: www.phdproject.org